The Basic Essentials of
TRAILSIDE SHELTERS
AND EMERGENCY SHELTERS

by Cliff Jacobson

Illustrations by
Cliff Moen

D1088566

ICS BOOKS, Inc.
Merrillville, Indiana

THE BASIC ESSENTIALS OF TRAILSIDE SHELTERS AND EMERGENCY SHELTERS

Copyright © 1992 Cliff Jacobson

10 9 8 7 6 5 4 3 2 1

Printed in U.S.A.

DEDICATION

To Darrell Foss, whose unwavering friendship has helped smooth the way through difficult times.

Published by:
ICS Books, Inc.
One Tower Plaza
107 E. 89th Avenue
Merrillville, IN 46410
800-541-7323

Library of Congress Cataloging-in-Publication Data

Jacobson, Cliff.
    The basic essentials of trail side shelters and emergency shelters
  / by Cliff Jacobson ; illustrations by Cliff Moen.
        p.   cm.
    Includes index.
    ISBN 0-934802-89-0 : $4.95
    1. Camping--Equipment and supplies. 2. Tents--Maintenance and repair. 3. Wilderness survival. I. Title. II. Title: Trail side shelters.
GV191.76.J33 1992
796.54'028--dc20   92-5191
                                                          CIP

TABLE OF CONTENTS

PREFACE

I recently read three wonderful old books which are long out-of-print. *Camping and Woodcraft,* by Horace Kephart, was published in 1917; *Woodcraft and Camping,* by "Nessmuk," appeared in 1920; and the Abercrombie (from Abercrombie and Fitch fame) camp catalog, circa 1912. Subtitled *Camp Outfits,* the 168 page Abercrombie catalog describes hundreds of then, state-of-the-art camping items. As I pored over the offerings in search of illuminating ideas for *Trail Shelters,* I discovered that the old-timers were just as concerned with product weight, bulk, and performance, as we are today. Consider Nessmuk's idea of a go-light outfit:

> During a canoe cruise across the Northern Wilderness in the late summer, I met many parties at different points in the woods, and the amount of unnecessary duffle with which they encumbered themselves was simply appalling. Why a shrewd business man, who goes through with a guide and makes a forest hotel his camping ground nearly every night should handicap himself with a five-peck pack basket full of gray woolen and gum blankets, extra clothing, pots, pans, and kettles, with a 9-pound 10-bore, and two rods—yes, and an extra pair of heavy boots hanging astride of the gun—well, it is one of the things I shall never understand. My own load, including canoe, extra clothing, blanket-bag, two days' rations, pocket-axe, rod and knapsack, never exceeded 26 pounds; and I went prepared to camp out in any weather and every night.

As Nessmuk unveils the mysteries of his go-light kit, he describes in great detail how to use every item in it—information frequently omitted from the pages of modern camping books. In fact, wilderness camping and canoeing were so popular in the 1920s, that *Forest and Stream* (forerunner of *Field & Stream*) magazine had a full time "canoe editor" on staff. When, a few years ago, I suggested that Field & Stream again address the "how to's" of outdoor living, they politely refused, saying that hunters and fishermen preferred the comforts of motels and RV's to the solitude of remote wilderness. Ditto for most self-propelled hikers and canoeists who also can't make a fire in driving rain, rig a snug tarp, sharpen a knife to a razor's edge, or complete a knot with a quick-release loop so it can be eliminated with a single pull. Kephart and Nessmuk understood quick-release (slippery) knots, and so did our pioneer ancestors. Check out the canvas shelters of the day, and you'll see that they knew geometry too. As I perused the Abercrombie catalog, I was amazed to discover that some surprisingly roomy two-person shelters weighed less than 5 pounds.

Contrary to popular belief, the old-timers were not bungling idiots who slashed and trashed the backcountry. They *knew* it took a long time to build a bough bed or a snug shelter, so they devised surprisingly good (and ecological) alternatives. For example, Kephart carried a one-pound mattress tick; Cal Rutstrum had a down-filled air mattress and "convertable A-tent." And every woodsman felt that a light canvas tarp was essential for rain—something modern voyagers still won't admit. If you asked a turn-of-the century woodsman for advice, he'd first tell you the method then suggest the equipment. Now, as every modern camper knows, the roles are completely reversed.

More often than not, today's outdoor "experts" rely on specialized equipment to cure their ills. For example, if rain gets inside your tent while you sleep, you are advised to buy a better tent. Chemical fire starters are the key to a cheery blaze in any weather, and polypropylene and pile clothing ensures your comfort in chilling rain. And if, dread of dreads, your worst equipment fears are realized, just crawl deep inside your waterproof/breathable sleeping bag until the foul weather passes. How perfectly awful. The old-timers would have been appalled.

Some years ago, after a protracted rain, I paddled my solo canoe quietly along the shore of Northern Lights Lake, on the edge of the Boundary Waters Canoe Area. Each camp I passed was a bedlam of clothes lines and drying gear—most of it modern nylon and polyester stuff. Round the bend, a smiling Scout troop was gathered by a roaring fire that was protected by a pair of tightly rigged canvas tarps. A nearly bare clothes line strung under the tarp suggested there was little wet clothing to dry. In the background I caught a glimpse of two well-pitched, forest-green canvas tents. The Scoutmaster waved me in for coffee, and I complied.

I learned that he had brought boys to this place every year for a decade. "The planning starts in the fall," he said. "We don't have much gear, but every Scout's 'first class' and knows the ropes." I studied the clean, well-managed camp and said, "I see."

The old backwoodsmen didn't relish pain, or being wet or cold or hungry. So they perfected their skills to the limits of their equipment. "A dry place to live and work out of the weather (read, rain tarp)" was the cornerstone of every turn-of-the-century camping book. And so too with *Trail Shelters*. In the pages that follow, we'll learn how to rig tarps and tents in a variety of configurations so they'll go up fast and remain standing in any wind or weather.

At a recent seminar, a man wryly suggested that my camping and canoeing ideas were old hat. "You've just taken the ideas of Nessmuk and Rutstrum and updated 'em," he said. "Shhhh," I replied. "Promise me you won't tell a soul!"

"When things become more important than skills."

1. TOOLS OF THE TRADE

When suddenly the sky turns black and the wind grows deadly still, you generally have only a few moments to pitch tents and get everything and everybody under a stormproof tarp. There's no time to cut hanks of line, fumble for tent stakes, poles, or groundsheets, or wonder where you put your pocket knife. Suddenly, your worst foul weather concerns have materialized.

You'll avoid much embarrassment when the weather turns sour if you gather these materials before you take to the woods:

    1.   One hundred feet of 1/8-inch diameter parachute cord for each tarp you plan to rig. Cut rope into 15-20-foot lengths and burn the ends so they

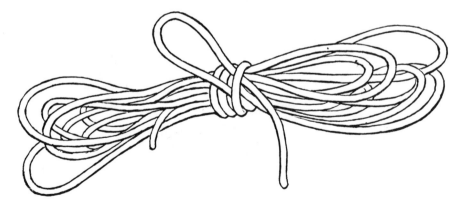

Figure 1-2   *Quick-release loop on hank of parachute cord.*

1

won't unravel. Then, tightly coil each hank and secure it with the quick-release loop illustrated in figure 1-2.

Tip: Choose brightly colored cord that you won't trip over in failing light.

2. Fifty feet of 1/4 or 3/16-inch diameter *braided* nylon rope (twisted rope unravels too easily) for each tarp. Singe the ends and coil the ropes by the method illustrated in figure 1-4.

3. Sharp knife. A handaxe and folding saw are also useful when you need to cut extension poles from dead, downed timber.

4. One or two waterproof nylon tarps (many of the shelters illustrated in this book require *two* paired tarps). The larger the tarp, the better. Eight by ten feet is about right for two. Ten by twelve or larger is best for four. Up to twelve people can comfortably crowd beneath two overlapped 12 x 12-foot rain flies. Customize your tarps as outlined in Chapter 3.

5. A small snow shovel and snow knife (a machete is perfect for the job). These are handy if you intend to build snow shelters. See chapter 8 for details.

6. Inexpensive plastic sheeting, which can be substituted for nylon tarps (please don't leave plastic in the woods) if you have "Vis-clamps" (ball and garter devices) or small rubber balls or pebbles. Figure 1-3 shows the attachment procedure.

7. Waterproof tape for making repairs to nylon and plastic.

You now have the essential tools needed to rig your shelters. Next step is to learn the knots and hitches which will hold them tight.

Figure 1-3   *Vis-clamp ball-and-garter device.*

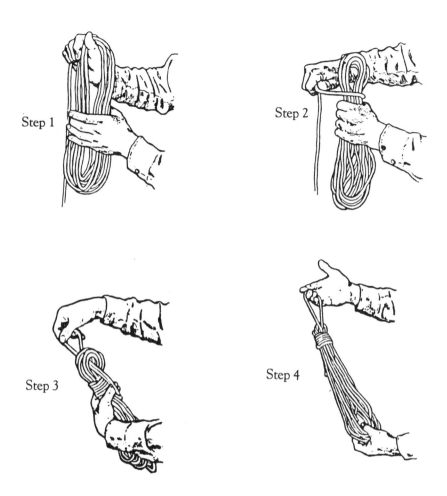

Step 1

Step 2

Step 3

Step 4

Step one—Coil the rope: take care to lay each coil carefully into place, twisting it a half turn so it will lay without twisting. Then, grasp the main body of the rope with one hand and place your thumb through the eye of the coils to hold them in place as shown above in step one.

Step two—Remove the last two coils of rope; take this long free end, and wind it around the main body of the rope several times. Wind the free end downward, toward the hand holding the rope body. Wind evenly and snugly. Don't make the coils too tight.

Step three—Form a loop with the free end of the rope as shown above in step three, and push it through the eye of the rope body.

Step four—Grasp the wound coils with one hand and the rope body with the other hand and slide the coils upward tightly against the loop. The rope is now coiled and secured (step four). Pulling the free end of the rope will release the line, which can quickly be make ready for throwing.

Figure 1-4 *Old navy method of coiling rope.*

2. ESSENTIAL KNOTS

While canoeing Manitoba's North Knife river in the summer of '91, my crew experienced three days of wind-driven, ice cold rain. Temperatures in the 30s and wind speeds of 30 miles an hour threatened to shred our paired (12' x 12') nylon rain tarps. I used every trick—and length of cord—to keep the shelter tight and well-drained.

When the skies cleared, we had one last admiring look at our storm-defying roof, before we began its disassembly. Resembling Charlotte's web, I'd used 200 feet of parachute cord, 100 feet of nylon rope, and two Prussik's to keep things taut. "Nice rig," remarked one man; "but how'll we ever get it down? Wet knots are murder to untie!"

"Just watch," I replied with a knowing grin. One pull of each "slippery" loop severed the lines in a matter of seconds. In all, barely five minutes were needed to coil ropes and cords and to stuff the flies into their awaiting sacks.

Fabric shelters must be tightly stressed to withstand high winds and prolonged rain. Guy and hem lines must be drum-tight yet undo easily (with a single pull) when the storm subsides. The alternative to quick-release knots is to pick, swear, and cut them apart. Experienced outdoors people always end their knots with the "slippery" loops illustrated in this chapter.

Outdoors handbooks define dozens of knots. But for camp use, the half-hitch, power-cinch, sheet-bend, and Prussik loop are enough. To this, add the shear and diagonal lashing, and you'll be prepared for any emergency.

Two Half-Hitches

Use two half-hitches to anchor a rope or cord to an immovable object like a tree or rock. Be sure to end the second half hitch with a quick-release loop as illustrated.

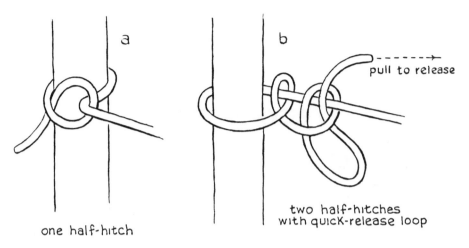

one half-hitch

two half-hitches
with quick-release loop

Figure 2-1   *Two half-hitches*

Power-Cinch

The power-cinch (a modification of the "trucker's knot") provides the block-and-tackle power you need to snug storm lines and keep them tight. It ties and unties in a flash and is much more powerful, secure, and versatile than the "tautline hitch" which is touted in old time camping books. See my book, *The Basic Essentials of Knots For the Outdoors*, for other practical uses of this ingenious hitch.

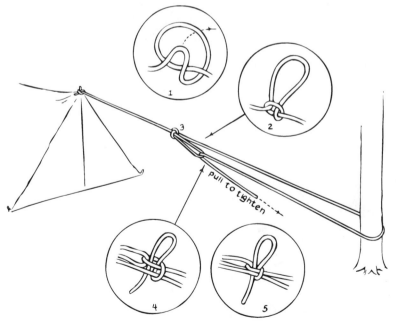

Figure 2-2   *Power-cinch*

Sheet-Bend

The sheet-bend is the knot of choice for tying two ropes together. Ropes tied with a sheet-bend won't slip under load, and they come apart easily even after being pelted by heavy rain. When rope sizes are dissimilar, use the *smaller diameter* rope to make the bend and quick-release feature.

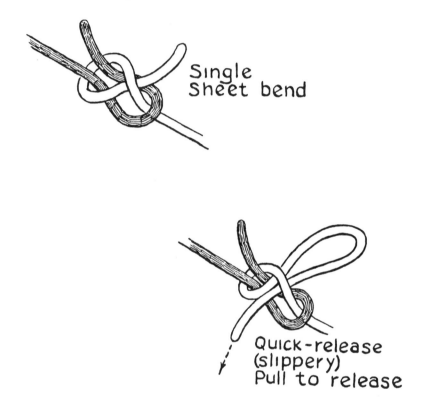

Single Sheet bend

Quick-release (slippery) Pull to release

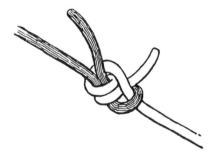

Double Sheet bend (for absolute security)

Figure 2-3   *Sheet-bend*

Prussik Loop

Scenario: Rain is pooling on a portion of your tarp. An aerial guy line would solve the problem but there is no place to anchor it. You could run a rope between two poorly situated trees then secure your guy line to it, but the pull would be parallel to the rope and the knot would slip down it. What to do?

Why, rig a Prussik loop, of course! Use the Prussik whenever you want an absolutely secure loop that won't slip along a tight line. Mountaineers use this knot for footholds to climb a vertical rope. The Prussik loop slides easily along a tight rope, yet it jams solidly when a horizontal or vertical load is applied. Make the loop from an 18-inch length of parachute cord completed with a sheet-bend.

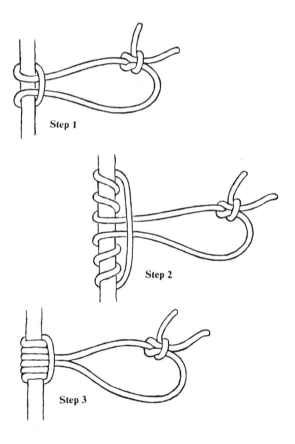

Figure 2-4 *Prussik loop*
Use the Prussik knot whenever you want an absolutely secure loop that won't slip along a tight line. Mountaineers use this knot to help them climb a vertical rope. I've found it's useful for rigging rainflies and for canoe rescue. Make a loop from a length of parachute cord, tied with a sheet-bend.

Lashings

Use a "modified" shear lashing to connect short spars together to achieve the pole length (around 6 feet) you need to heighten the roof of a rain tarp. A diagonal lashing will connect spars in an "X" configuration and allow you to erect a tight ridge line when rope is in short supply.

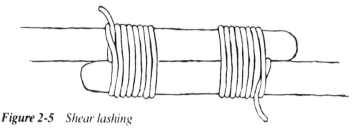

Figure 2-5   *Shear lashing*

Modified Shear Lashing

Place the poles parallel to one another and tie a clove hitch around one pole. Then, wind your cord tightly around both poles several times and finish with a clove hitch .

Diagonal Lashing

Begin with a very tight timber hitch around both poles. Take three or four turns side-by-side around one fork, and three or four more side-by-side around the other. Then, tighten the lashing with two frapping turns and end it with a clove hitch around one of the poles.

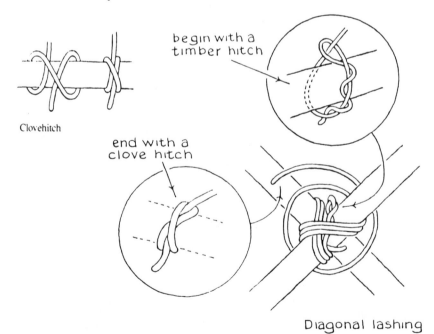

Clovehitch

begin with a timber hitch

end with a clove hitch

Diagonal lashing

Figure 2-6   *Diagonal lashing*

3. TARP TRICKS

Given the choice between camping with a small tent and large rain tarp or a large tent and no tarp, I'll take the former every time. When rain-bound minutes turn to hours (or days), you'll relish the chance to leave your confining shelter, stretch, and do chores without being pelted by the elements. A tightly strung, well-drained fly (tarp) provides the protection you need to work outside. As the ladies and gentlemen of American Express say, "Don't leave home without it!"

No need to purchase expensive tarps (I suggest you get two). Any waterproof nylon—ripstop or taffeta—is fine. Most factory tarps come with grommets which rip out after a few good storms. Customize your tarp(s) according to the illustration below. Two hours time and a light duty sewing machine are all you need.

Tip: Well-sewn nylon loops (get inch-wide nylon webbing at any camping shop) are *much more* reliable than grommets. If you're a belt-and-suspenders person, you'll replace critically located corner grommets with well-reinforced nylon loops. Allow no more than 12 inches of space between loops or grommets. Be sure to back whatever you sew with heavy material.

Sew a 6-inch square "pole patch" of heavy material to the inside center (opposite the center guy line) of your fly. This will allow you to use an interior center pole when there are no trees to which you can attach an outside guy line. Nylon stretches and abrades easily, so a reinforcing patch is essential if you plan to use a pole.

Attach loops of parachute cord to each grommet or loop. Loops should be large enough to allow insertion of a wire stake. Leave at least 6-inches of "tie" hanging, as illustrated.

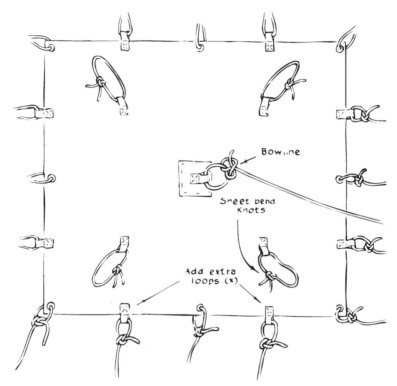

Figure 3-1   *Customized tarp*

Tip: Braided nylon cord holds knots better than the inexpensive, sheathed parachute cord sold at hardware stores.

Attach generously-sized chute cord loops to each of the five webbed loops on the face of the fly. Loops should be tied with a sheetbend. One 20-foot long cord should be permanently secured to the *center* face loop.

Finally, waterproof all seams. I prefer Thompson's Water Seal—an industrial strength compound used for sealing wood and concrete block. TWS won't crack and peel in winter or get sticky in July. Two applications, spaced an hour apart, provide life-long protection. Apply the product sparingly with a foam varnish brush. Use TWS on your tent seams, maps, and journals, too. Every hardware store has it.

When thunderheads loom threateningly overhead and the wind builds to impressive speeds, you generally have only a few minutes to rig a stormproof camp. So keep everything you need to rig your tarp—50-foot rope, five, 20-foot coils of parachute cord, and six stakes—in a nylon stuff sack with cordlock closure.

Tip: Stuff your fly, don't roll it. Stuffing is faster and easier on the waterproof coating. Be certain everything is bone dry before you pack it away.

Dampness provides a media for microorganisms to attack the waterproof polyurethane coating on the fly. Microbes will not attack nylon, but they *will* devour the polyurethane coating on it. Ever see a tent floor whose waterproof coating has peeled? More than likely the tent was put away wet.

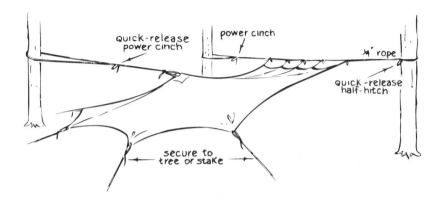

Figure 3-2 *Single lean-to "meat-and-potatoes" rig.*

Single Lean-To Rig

This "meat-and-potatoes" configuration can be erected alone in about three minutes and will withstand winds of 30 miles an hour. The sloping design spills water effectively and conserves the warmth of a reflector fire.

The procedure for assembly is as follows:

1. Locate two trees about 15 feet apart and string a drum-tight line between them, about 5 feet off the ground. Use two quick-release half-hitches at one end and a quick-release power-cinch at the other.
2. Take the pair of ties at one corner of the fly and tightly wind one tie of the set clockwise around the rope. Wind the other tie counter-clockwise. Take at least four turns around the rope then secure the ties with an overhand bow.
3. Pull the other corner of the open end of the fly tight along the rope and secure it with the ties, winding them around the rope, as above. The tie wrappings will provide tension to keep the corners of the tarp from slipping inward along the rope when the fly is buffeted by wind.
4. Secure all remaining ties to the rope with a simple overhand bow. Note that by securing the fly at several points along the length of its open end rather than just at the corners, you distribute the strain across a wide area, thus increasing the strength of the fly. High wind will tear out the corner grommets or loops unless you distribute the load along a main hem line, as illustrated.
5. Pull the back of the fly out tight and stake it.

Figure 3-3 *Back-logged fire*

6. Run the center cord over a tree limb or a horizontal rope strung above and behind the fly. Snug the cord and secure it with a quick-release power-cinch. Use an interior center pole (a canoe paddle propped on a pack works well if trees are not available). Connect additional lines (use a quick-release sheet-bend) to other face loops as needed to produce drum-tight geometry.

   In ultra-high winds, guy or stake the side hems of the fly to the ground or adjacent trees.

   A fire built just under the open edge of the fly will provide substantial heat inside the lean-to. However, since the fly acts as a "wind eddy," you must backlog your fire or it will smoke you out. The bottom of an aluminum canoe works well, as does a large sheet of aluminum foil. You can even use several packs if you keep them *well away* from the flames. The real purpose of the backing is to draw smoke away from the enclosure, not reflect heat into it. Note that the fire must be completely *outside* the tarp. The backlogs have insufficient area to make up for the size of the wind eddy created by the huge tarp.

   When rigging twin tarps, you can foil the smoke with the ingenious procedure illustrated in figure 3-4.

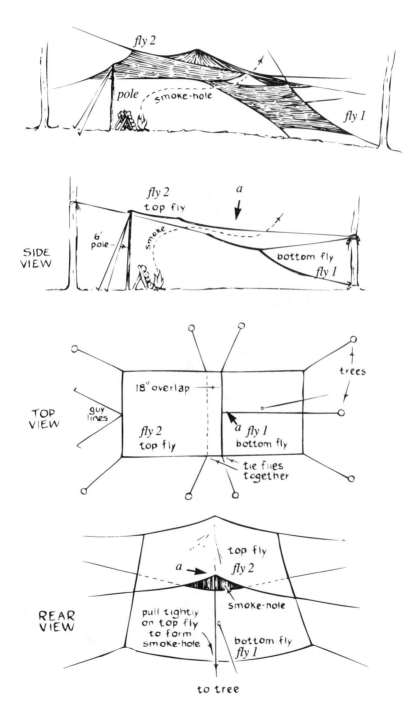

Figure 3-4   *Twin flies; slanted one floated, fire out front and smoke vented.*

Twin Flies With Fire Slit

Here's a secure, airy shelter that will provide luxurious comfort for up to 12 people. Two people can rig it in about 10 minutes, even in high winds. You'll need two 10' x 12' "customized" flies and all your rope and cord.

Beauty of this arrangement is that you can build a rain-protected warming fire right underneath the fly. The combination backlog and overhead vent spills smoke through the opening on top. You can "float" the slanted roof, as illustrated, to provide more interior room, or stake it to the ground for protection from blowing wind.

The procedure for assembly is as follows:

1. Rig the single lean-to configuration shown in figure 3-2. In vertical rains, "float" the back as illustrated in figure 3-4. Remember to connect all lines to one another with a quick-release sheet-bend.
2. Overlap to the second grommet the hem of fly #2 over the hem of fly #1. This should provide an approximate 2-foot overlap. Then, secure the corner ties of fly #2 to the ties on the side hem of fly #1.
3. Attach a 20-foot length of chute cord to the center grommet of fly #2 (point "a" in figure 3-4) and secure this cord to a tree—or line strung between two trees—directly behind fly #1. If you won't build a fire under fly #2, you may guy this line to a stake at the base of fly #1.
4. Cut a sturdy, 6-foot long pole from dead, downed wood, or use a shear lashing to extend several short spars to this length. Tie the top of the pole to the center ties on fly #2. Run twin guylines from the pole tip to the stakes below. Secure guylines with a power-cinch. Stake or guy out the corners of fly #2.
5. Go to the back of fly #1 and tighten the overhead "vent" cord ("a") until the structure is tight. There should be an approximate 6-inch gap between the overlapped portions of the two flies. Last step is to add additional storm lines on the face and hem of both flies to produce a taut shape that won't pool water.

You now have a huge, sturdy shelter that won't pool water or flap in the wind.

With the exception of the special purpose barrenland rig illustrated in figure 3-9 the shelters illustrated in figures 3-2 and 3-4 should satisfy all your needs.

Camp Fire Considerations

Build the fire just inside the hem of fly#2. Backlog it as explained. Smoke will follow the backlogged eddy line to the roof of fly #2 and be drawn out through the slit between the two flies. This works slick when there's no wind. You'll have to experiment a bit here as a good breeze may confuse the eddies and allow the shelter to fill with smoke. You will also discover that if you raise the back of fly #1 off the ground to provide more headroom, the bottom draft that results will pull smoke away from the vent and into the shelter. Ingenuity and strong backlogging will usually solve most smoke problems.

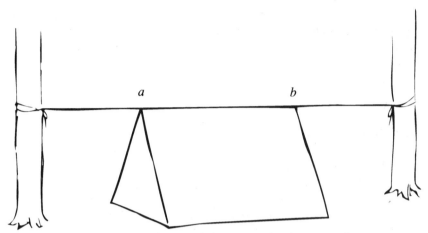

Figure 3-5a *a) A-Frame: Classic tight line set-up that doesn't work.*

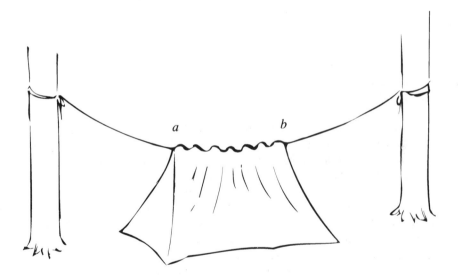

Figure 3-5b *Note how material bunches along catenary curve.*

A-Frame

Old-time camping books suggest the arrangement shown in figure 3-5a, which looks better on paper than on the ground. That's because a tightly drawn rope follows a "catenary" curve, and material draped over it bunches up along the middle. Good tents are patterned at the ridge to account for this natural droop, whereas cheap tents rely on aluminum ridge poles or shockcord to keep things tight.

When using a "ridge cord," you must pull out the extreme ends ("a" and "b") of the fly and tie them to the rope (take several wraps around it) as in step 2 of "rigging a single lean-to." Better yet, forget the ridge line and tie individual cords directly to the tarp at points "a" and "b." In either case, the result is a floppy but useable shelter.

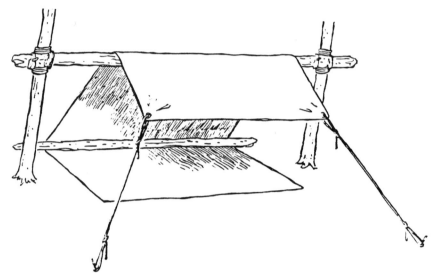

Figure 3-6   *Open A-Frame*

Some camping texts suggest that you substitute a pole for the rope ridge— practical only if you have a *smooth* piece of wood that won't abrade the fly. Even then, it's a time-consuming rig—one which may require crossed spars at the ends (or multiple guylines) to support the wooden ridge pole.

Open A-Frame

The "open a-frame" is practical if you have a straight, smooth pole and closely spaced trees to support it. The stiff ridge pole withstands heavy snow loads, and the sharply sloping backside of the lean-to effectively sheds snow. Here again, finding a smooth straight ridge pole is tougher than you think.

Square Sheet Lean-To (See Figure 3-7)

The "square sheet lean-to" is a very wind-stable design that effectively absorbs heat from a backlogged fire. An even more rigid shelter can be constructed from a triangular (equilateral) shaped piece of material. Tie the fly to the pole at points "a" and "b," then peg out the base at the corners and midpoints. Secure the vertical spars with a diagonal lashing.

Canoe Prop Method (See Figure 3-8)

Prop a canoe on paddles and cover it with your rain tarp, as shown in figure 3-8. If you have two canoes, prop them side-by-side about 6-feet apart, parallel to one .another and cover them with a tarp. Stake and guy the tarp and push out the center with a paddle so it won't pool water. *Don't trust this set-up in a strong wind.*

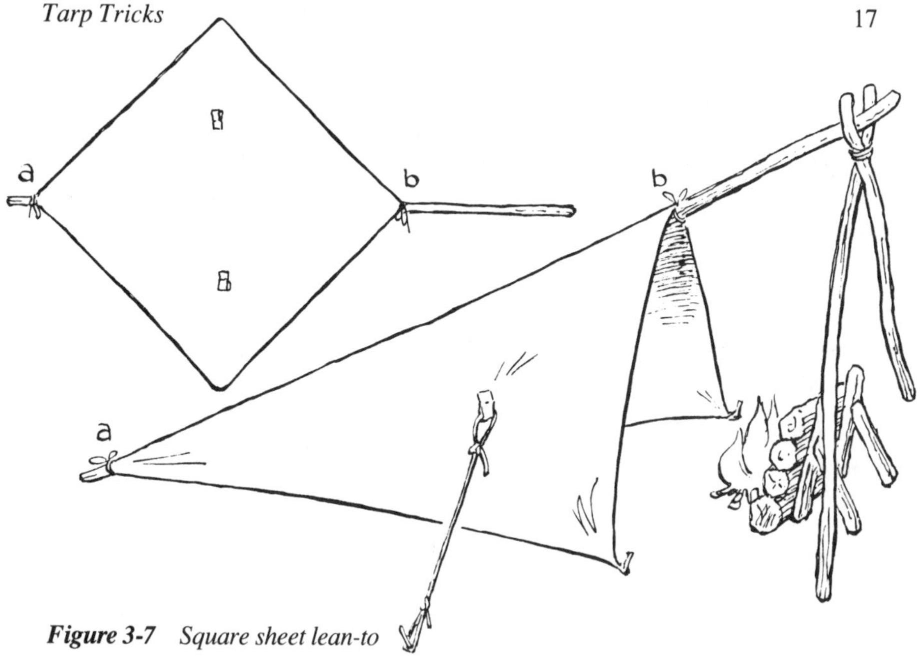

Figure 3-7 *Square sheet lean-to*

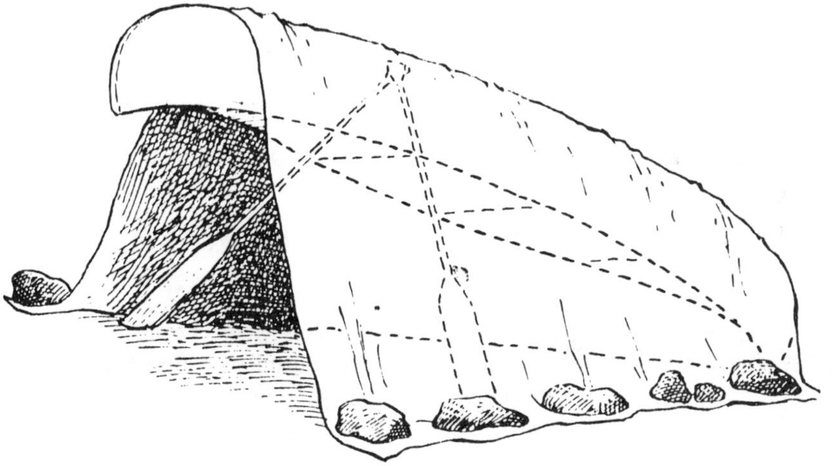

Figure 3-8 *Canoe prop*
Use this method to prop-up two canoes side by side. One canoe can provide instant shelter with the use of a tarp.

If it's *perfectly calm*, you can prop up the back ends of the canoes, as well as the front, to produce a non-sloping shelter with more interior space.

I don't like the "canoe prop" method. It's hard on paddles and not very secure. But it is useful in light rain and handy when you need protection for a small fire.

Tip: A single "canoe prop" without fly makes a quick shelter for two in a

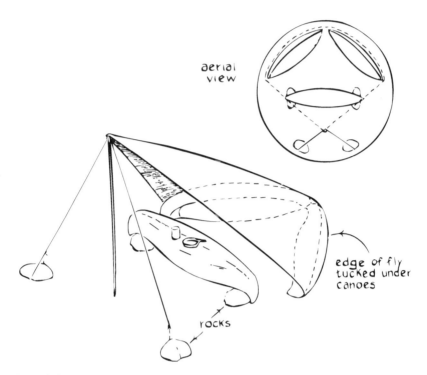

aerial
view

edge of fly
tucked under
canoes

rocks

Figure 3-9   *Twin canoe tundra rig ("QUICK RIG TUNDRA TARP").*

light, vertical rain. I've used it many times to prepare lunch along a portage trail on a rainy day.

Quick Rig Tundra Tarp

Scenario: You're canoeing in the barren lands where no trees and high winds are the rule. Rig a "canoe prop," like that illustrated in figure 3-8, and it will go sailing off into the tundra before you can move in. What to do? Why, use your canoes to weight the tarp, of course. And oh yes, you'll need one 5 to 7-foot aluminum pole.

The procedure for assembly is as follows:

1. Lay the tarp flat on the ground and weight two adjacent sides with over-turned canoes.
2. Hoist the apex of the shelter on a long pole then guy the pole and remaining loose fabric in place. Total rigging time? Less than three minutes.

Tip: You can construct a more spacious shelter by placing the canoes inside the fly, bellies facing the occupants. Drape the tarp partially over the canoes and tie it to them (you'll need several short lengths of cord).

Tip: An overturned canoe blocked up on the sides makes a great table. Remove the side blocks and it becomes a windbreak for your stove.

Single-Walled Desert SunTeepee

Similar to the "quick rig tundra tarp" illustrated in figure 3-9, the sun teepee requires one pole and one guyline. For a taut configuration, you'll need to guy out the mid-point of the fly—impossible if there are no trees. However, stacking gear against the inside back wall will stiffen the shelter considerably.

As you can see, there are dozens of ways to rig tarps. And that's the problem. Most people are so baffled by all the possible configurations that they never master a single design. My advice? Forget about the cute options suggested in survival texts and become expert at rigging the "single lean-to" and "twin flies with fire slit". For desert or barren land camping, the "quick rig tundra tarp" or its derivative, the "single-walled sun teepee," is most practical.

4. YOUR TENT—THE ULTIMATE TRAIL SHELTER

And the night shall be filled with music
And the cares that infest the day,
Shall fold their tents like Arabs
And as silently steal away.
    Henry Wadsworth Longfellow
    from *A Psalm of Life*.

It's been four hours now and still it continues. The water comes in sheets, cold and unrelenting. Everywhere, the ground is drenched with it; every rut holds a pool, every leaf a tiny pond. Contentedly, you peer through the mosquito net of your nylon tent at the vastness of the forest beyond. The sky, deep gray and forboding, communicates that "more of the same" is on the way.

20

Overhead, a small aluminum candle lantern provides some warmth and enough light to permit reading a novel. You laze against the loosely rolled sleeping bag and momentarily stare into the dampness of the day. A smug smile flashes briefly: granted, the 5 x 7-foot A-Frame tent is a bit cramped for two. But no matter; it is warm and dry. Be it ever so humble, there is no place like home, even when it is a confining backpack tent pitched on a secluded ridge deep in the Adirondacks.

Five states to the west, a similar scenario is in progress. A man, woman, 12-year-old girl, and tow-headed boy of nine peer wistfully through the netted window of their spacious 9-foot square umbrella tent. The walls of the 10-ounce canvas Eureka rustle contentedly to the rhythm of the wind-whipped rain. Outside, tiny icicles drip from the well-bronzed canvas, but inside, warmed by the glow of a Coleman lantern, it is snug and dry. The 6-foot peak provides plenty of room to stand and dress, and the spacious floor plan encourages games and socializing. This family has been confined for six hours, but they are having a very good time. Yet, all around, far as the eye can see, the KOA campground is deserted. Where, earlier, dozens of tents had dotted the treeless field, now, there is only grass and rain. Everyone else has gone—casualties of the persistent rain.

At the top of the continent, just above the Arctic Circle, two canoe campers ride out a polar gale in their low slung geodesic dome. The state-of-the-art nylon igloo expands and contracts with every gust of the 50 mile per hour wind, but it holds firm. Thirty-six hours later, two smiling voyagers emerge onto the still, sunlit tundra, grateful that their tent had weathered the storm.

As you can see, there is no such thing as a perfect tent, or even an all-round one. What's best for car-camping is out-of-place in the tundra or on the hiking trail. Backpacking in the mountains is not like desert hiking or wilderness canoeing. And winter camping imposes new demands. Tents designed to withstand high winds may perform poorly in rain, and vice versa. Those built to withstand snow loads may be too heavy or difficult to pitch. Ones light enough to carry long distances may test your sanity on a rainy day, while larger models may strain the confines of your backpack. And so it goes. When you do find your dream tent it may simply cost too much.

But don't despair; there is order in the universe. The following principles of tent design and construction will help you separate the wheat from the chaff. Figure 4-2 will help you with terminology.

Design And Construction Features

It's fashionable in magazines to get as technical as possible when describing the design and construction of a given product. Tents are no exception. I could easily bore you with statistics about the warp and weave of various fabrics, the comparative strengths of aluminum, fiberglass, and carbon-fiber alloy poles, the advantages of one thread type over another, and so on. But the truth is that construction features are vastly over-rated. Commotion about thread count, number of stitches per inch, reinforcement of zipper ends and such, proudly touted by tent makers, takes a back seat to *good design*—a feature not always associated with quality construction or high price. In all my years of canoeing and camping, I've never seen a well-designed

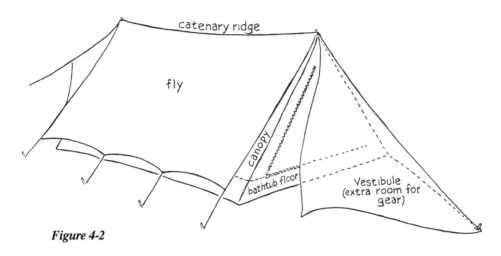

Figure 4-2

tent come apart at the seams or a zipper rip from its stitching. But I've experienced enough bent poles, torn flies, and broken zippers to know that fabrics and sloppy sewing are rarely the villains.

In the pages that follow, we'll explore the factors which contribute to the making of a good tent. If you keep uppermost in your mind that good design, impeccable construction, and high price, don't always go hand-in-hand, you'll be well on your way to finding the ideal tent for your purposes and pocketbook.

Design Principles

If you asked a boating expert how to tell a seaworthy canoe from one that's not, he or she might use this analogy:

Pretend your hands are water and place them on the keel-line of the canoe. Now, slide your hands up towards the rails. Is there substantial flare here? Good. Water will follow that flare away from the hull rather than into it. But if your hands "tumble home" (follow the inward curve of the canoe above the waterline), water will do the same. It's no mystery why flare-sided dories are more seaworthy than hard-chined rowboats.

Now try this same test on your tent. Follow the fly to the ground, as if your hands were water. Do your hands fall on unprotected seams? If so, rain will pool here and seep into your tent. And seam-sealant (glue) won't keep you dry for very long. The most reliable way to keep seams from leaking is to cover them with waterproof material. A fly that *stakes right to the ground* will do the trick, but few tents come so equipped. To save weight, many tents have short "cap" flies which don't protect the canopy in wind-driven rain. If you have a tent that is built this way and plan to use it in high winds, you should extend the fly by sewing on waterproof material. Again, let me emphasize that seam-sealant is a make-shift solution to a bad design. *Note:* Some sophisticated mountaineering tents now feature machine sealed (heat tape) seams like those applied to the best rainwear. These seams won't leak in any weather.

Exceptions aside, you are best advised to avoid any tent that has perimeter seams which are not fully covered by the fly. The floors of some tents, like the Eureka Timberline, are sewn to the canopy several inches above ground. This *bathtub* construction puts vulnerable seams under the protection of the fly where they belong. All the best rain tents have *bathtub floors*.

Now, check the tent corners where the floor seams and door zippers come together. Does the fly drip water onto any stitching? If so, find a way to fix it or keep shopping.

The entrance and window(s) are other critical components. Are there generously-sized awnings over doors and vents to keep rain out? Are exterior zippers protected by weather flaps? Can you easily turn aside a weather flap with your hand? If so, wind will do the same. Many of the best tents use elastic or Velcro to keep weather flaps in place. Perhaps you can make modifications.

Vestibules are worth their weight in gold on a rainy day. They function as an extra room to store packs and wet gear. More importantly, they protect the entrance (all those exposed seams and zippers we are concerned about) against blowing wind and rain, and they provide a place to cook out-of-the-weather when you're too lazy to rig a rain tarp. Vestibules are generally add-on affairs which secure to the tent canopy with clips, shockcord and the like. One ingenious tent, the Cannondale Aroostook, comes with *two* integral vestibules—a good idea. Backpackers, canoeists, bikers, and others who require light, rainproof tents will *demand* a vestibule.

Geometry

There are A-Frames, teepees, tunnels, domes, lean-to's, and sophisticated geometric shapes that defy description.

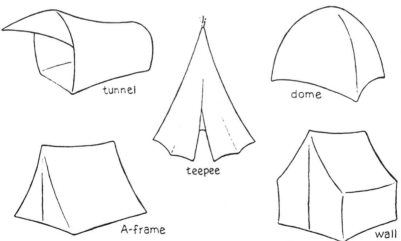

Figure 4-3 *Tent Style: a-frame, tunnel, dome teepee, wall tent.*

Domes

Space-wise, domes are the most efficient of tent designs. The high, gradually sloping sidewalls of a dome provide a pleasant spacious atmosphere, and the hexagon- or octagon-shaped floor permits occupants to sleep in any direction—a real advantage if the tent is pitched "wrong" or on a sloping site.

Domes have faults. Though they shed rain efficiently, they're badly ventilated (the fly covers the windows and door) and not very wind-stable. *Geodesic* domes, which utilize a lattice of arrow-shaft aluminum poles, are the exception. However, serious geodesic designs are time-consuming to pitch and *very* expensive. All domes (geodesics included) crush in extremely high winds unless they are well guyed and staked. This means running storm lines through slits in the fly to guy points on the poles. Rigging a dome for gale-force winds is quite a task, though once accomplished, the tent will hold.

By design, domes cannot utilize *bathtub floor* construction. The many-faceted floor must be sewn to the canopy at ground level, which leaves plenty of seams for you to glue. Ironically, some of the best domes have short flies which leave perimeter floor seams exposed to the weather. Such construction can result in a sponge party in prolonged rain.

Geodesic domes were designed as mountaineering tents. Since they're basically free-standing, can be shoved into small crevices, and don't need to be rotated to face into a changing wind, they are ideal for situations where creature comfort, light weight, small packed size, and wind-stability are important factors.

Teepees

"You have noticed, " said Black Elk, "that everything an Indian does is in a circle and that is because the power of the world works in circles and everything tries to be round. The life of man is a circle from childhood to childhood. Our tipi's were round, like the nests of birds. But the white men have put us in square boxes. It is a bad way to live for there can be no power in a square."

John Neihardt, Black Elk Speaks

(from *THE TENT BOOK*, by E.M. Hatton, 1979, Houghton Mifflin Co.)

The teepee is perhaps the most efficient and ingenious of tent designs. No other tent of comparable size sheds wind and rain as well, is as cool in summer, as warm in winter, and as versatile. The American Indian knew what he was doing when he designed the teepee.

Indian teepees are actually egg-shaped, not round as is commonly believed. The long axis of the cone was placed windward to brace the structure against the harsh prairie winds. Ventilation was provided by the doorway and a clever system of flaps at the apex. In winter, fine brush (insulation) was stacked between the inner tent liner and outer wall. It was all very ingenious and difficult to improve upon.

The modern nylon teepee is a far cry from its skin-covered ancestor. Three aluminum poles provide support, and a removable cap fly keeps out the weather. Entry is a zippered door or traditional hole.

Teepees light enough for backpacking share the same wet-weather inadequacies as domes, but they're more rigid and so remain rock-solid in winds that would flatten conventional tents of equal height. However, their flies are slow and awkward to install and have stakes and guylines everywhere, and there is no awning over the doorway to keep rain out. Teepees are great for semi-permanent camps. Otherwise, forget 'em.

Tunnels

Tunnels are low-to-the-ground affairs which are supported by a network of semi-rigid aluminum hoops. Designed for severe service, tunnels are among the most wind-stable tents. Their small size makes them light and compact. Inside, they are cramped and dog-housey, but they're generally more rain-proof and better ventilated than domes. For high altitude work and where weight is critical, they have few peers.

A-Frames

A-Frames are by far your best buy. These tents shed rain and wind effectively, allow construction of water-resistant bathtub floors and protective awnings, are well-ventilated and pest-proof, and are less costly to manufacture than other styles. In its most elementary form (a single I-pole at each end), the A-Frame is the lightest, most compact, and strongest of all tents. The design is thousands of years old but it is still a good one.

Umbrellas

Umbrella tents are traditional for family camping. And for good reason. They go up easily on any terrain and are almost entirely self-supporting. There's standing room inside and a generous awning out front under which to cook and relax. With full-length flies, these tents are rain and windproof.

The umbrella design is not just for family tents. Some very sophisticated backpacking tents—like the Eureka Equinox—are currently being built on this pattern.

Fabrics

Nylon is the most suitable fabric for light weight backpacking tents. Cotton tents are too heavy and bulky for most forms of self-propelled travel. Nylon tents need a porous canopy to let body-produced moisture out, and a protective waterproof fly to prevent rain from getting in. Check the fit between fly and canopy: the two must not touch at any point (even when stressed by high wind), or condensation and dripping will result.

Hardware and Amenities

Poles should be *aluminum*, no and's or if's! There is no such thing as a good fiberglass or plastic composite pole. *Wands* (not supporting members) which are used to hold out awnings and vents are an exception, though even here, aluminum is better. It follows that large-diameter aluminum poles of equivalent alloy are less apt to break than smaller poles. I prefer 0.75-inch diameter, tempered poles if I can get them. Thin, arrow-shaft poles are fine, if there are enough of them. All poles should be shock-corded for easy assembly.

U-pound 'em stakes are the pits. Except in sand and snow, heavy duty, 10-inch aluminum skewers are best.

Tip: Eight-inch aluminum concrete nails make acceptable low cost tent stakes.

Bug netting may be standard mosquito type or "no-see-um" proof. I prefer the former as it is stronger, easier to see through, and allows free flow of air. Tightly woven no-see-um-proof netting can be stifling on hot nights. When the tiny gnats begin their act, simply spray your mosquito net with bug dope, or close the fabric door panel.

A well-designed tent has the door panel inside the bug net so you can open the door to peek out *without* unzipping the screen.

Some tents have "niceties" like lantern loops and inside pockets for the storage of small items. These features—which require only a few minutes on a sewing machine to make—add considerable cost to a tent without significantly increasing its utility.

Packing Your Tent

Lightweight backpacking tents are designed to pack small. However, the poles are usually an obnoxious contender. Most pole sections are too long—24

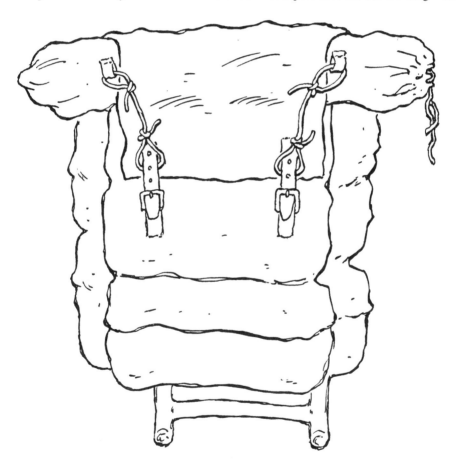

Figure 4-4   *Tent pole bag secured beneath modern packsack flap.*

inches or so—to fit crossways inside a modern backpack. So hikers commonly place the long tent bag under the closing flap of their packsack which exposes it to the elements and thorny vegetation. Far better to pack tent and poles separately, as follows:

1. Stuff or roll the tent *without stakes and poles* and place it in a nylon bag. Pack poles and stakes in a separate bag with drawstring closure.
2. Pack the tent *inside* your waterproof pack, out of contact with the elements.
3. Set the pole and stake bag under the pack flap and run the closing straps of the pack flap through loops of nylon cord sewn to the ends of the pole bag. Cinch the pack flap down tightly; the nylon cords will keep the pole bag from sliding out beneath the pack flap.

Selecting A Family Tent

My family's first camping tent was a 9' x 9' umbrella model with a wet wax finish, a steel telescoping center pole, and two netted windows with flaps that tied shut. It weighed 52 pounds and when rolled, barely fit into the trunk of the car. In hot weather, it smelled like kerosine and paraffin, and in rain, it leaked profusely. But it was inexpensive, and it enabled us to see a lot of country on not a lot of money.

Family tents, like the times, have changed. They've gotten more expensive, of course, but they're also lighter, stronger, roomier, and more weatherproof than those of the sixties. And they're easier to pitch too. Guylines are passe, as are obtrusive center poles and odors. Ties have been replaced by nylon zippers and Velcro, and shock-corded aluminum poles have succeeded steel ones. Even the largest family tents can be erected in less than 10 minutes.

For comfort, you need at least 21 square feet of floor space per person, more than that if you use cots. Tents with rectangular floors use space more efficiently than those with square or circular floors, which means more room between sleepers.

Weight

Three to 4 pounds per person is the rule for lightweight backpacking tents; 5 to 6 pounds for canoeing and high altitude expedition tents, and up to 10 pounds for drag-'em-out-of-the-car family shelters. Many of the best tents weigh much less than this.

Height

Waiting out a rain in a tent you can't stand in is no fun. However, low profile tents with sloping sides spill wind better than high-sided umbrella and wall tents, so you may have to make some sacrifices if you camp where there are big winds.

Fabrics

Though nylon is the most popular and best fabric for the construction of small tents, lightweight cotton is still a good choice for family tents where weight is less of a concern. It's impractical to use double-walled (waterproof fly/porous canopy) construction in large tents, so one layer of waterproof nylon is usually used throughout—a design that encourages condensation inside. Big windows and a porous cotton or nylon roof help dispel some moisture but not enough to prevent these tents from occasionally turning into saunas.

Nonetheless, if you confine your trips to areas where high humidity and rain are infrequent, then you may like an all nylon tent. In any case, be sure the tent has at least two rain-protected windows. The best nylon family tents have four-way ventilation—three windows and a door.

Speed of pitching

A tent that requires 10 minutes to pitch in dry, windless weather may require twice that long to erect in a rain storm. It's faster to assemble poles than to drive stakes and tie guylines, so choose a tent that is supported mainly by poles.

Modesty curtains

Family tents are commonly used in areas where there are other campers, so they should be designed to provide privacy without sacrificing ventilation. Some tents have a "modesty curtain"—a short fabric panel that attaches behind the door—in addition to the regular entry flap. On hot days you can leave the door open for ventilation and close the modesty curtain for privacy.

Clothing loops

Convenience dictates plenty of D-rings, loops, or brass hooks at the ridge to hang wet towels, clothing, and your battery-powered lantern. Warning: Mantel lanterns put out enough heat to burn through the roof of flame-retardant tents. And they consume lots of precious oxygen as they produce poisonous carbon monoxide. For this reason, you should hang only *flameless* lanterns inside your tent. Heaters, except catalytic ones, are also unsafe in tents.

Winter Tents

Most travelers use their three-season nylon tent for snow camping, which works well enough if they rig a *frost liner* inside. A piece of cotton sheeting, hung from the roof by ties or Velcro, absorbs exhaled moisture that might condense and freeze on the sleeping bags below.

A more gracious style of winter camping, which was popular a century ago, is again finding favor among those who spend long periods of time in the wilds. A 7' x 9' or larger canvas tent is rigged to accept a small sheet metal stove and pipe. A generously-sized canvas fly defies blowing rain, increases interior temperatures, and protects the roof from sparks. The tent *must* be canvas. Hot sparks will melt nylon instantly and cause serious burns! Most winter campers use wall tents or vintage Eureka Drawtights. Authentic period canvas tents—some of which are wonderful for this sort of thing—are available from TENTSMITHS, Box 496, North Conway, NH 03860 (603-447-2344). Write for their catalog.

In summary, the best tents are largely self-supporting and have full-length flies and bathtub floors that wrap well up the sidewalls. Protective awnings over doors and windows are a must, as are heat-treated aluminum poles and one or more vestibules.

Tent Care

New canvas tents should be tightly pitched and hosed down with water so they'll shrink evenly and become watertight. Never use soap, detergents, or bleach (horrors) on a cotton tent: it may damage the canvas and/or dissolve the waterproofing compound. Nylon tents require no care other than an occasional surface cleaning with a sponge and water. Ground-in dirt may be removed with soap and water. Avoid use of harsh detergents and solvents.

Store tents in a porous cotton or nylon sack. Be sure the bag is large enough. A dry, properly rolled tent that "fills its sack" when dry won't fit when it's soaked with rain.

Never roll and store a wet tent. Even rot-resistant nylon tents are sewn with cotton/Dacron™ thread which can mildew. As mentioned, damp polyurethane coatings provide food for microorganisms.

Tent seams should be waterproofed so they won't leak. Thompson's Water Seal works great on cotton and nylon.

A whisk broom and small sponge will keep your tent clean and neat. Never store a tent on concrete or leave it exposed to sunlight for extended periods.

5. STORMPROOFING YOUR TENT

A sewing machine and 60 minutes are all you need to turn your tent into a bombproof shelter!

Scenario: You pitch your tent—a four person Eureka! Timberline on a gentle knoll near a clump of youthful birch trees. There's a better spot 20 feet away—a well worn area where hundreds of tents have stood before. But there's a slight depression here; a good rain could flood you out. And nearby, is a long dead spruce, its limbs poised menacingly overhead, waiting patiently for a high wind to send it crashing down.

Slowly it begins with the tap tap of intermittent rain. Then it intensifies into unrelenting drizzle. For awhile, you stand complacently in the gentle shower and curiously watch the blackening clouds approach. Then you suddenly awaken to the realization that you have only a few minutes to get things under control before the storm unleashes its fury.

First, you string two parachute cord guylines from each peak to stakes below. Next, you weight the corner stakes with rocks then turn your attention to the right sidewall which is being crushed by the building wind. It would be nice if you could turn the tent into the storm, but the site won't cooperate. Besides, it's too late now; you'll have to make do by shoring up the windward sidewall and poles. You're glad now that you sewed storm-line pull-outs to the fly before you left home. As the wall firms under these tight guylines, you wonder why they aren't standard equipment on every tent.

Satisfied now that everything's secure, you retire to the tent, confident you'll stay dry no matter how hard it rains.

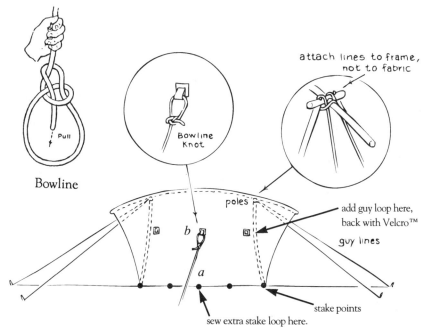

Bowline

attach lines to frame, not to fabric

Bowline Knot

Pull

poles

add guy loop here, back with Velcro™

guy lines

b

a

stake points

sew extra stake loop here.

Figure 5-1 *Eureka rigged with twin lines at peak, storm line on mid-sections.*

Philosophy

Admittedly, staying dry in a deluge requires luck as well as skill. What would you have done if there had been no well-drained spot? Or if rocks or uncooperative ground kept you from placing your tent where you wanted? And don't forget that clump of birch you used for a windscreen.

Nonetheless, even a bad campsite can be made habitable if you correct the shortcomings of your tent and follow these rules.

The Right Spot

Every camping book contains advice on "choosing the right campsite"—wasted rhetoric, for even a rank novice can tell a good spot from a bad one. However, it's unethical (and often illegal) to clear trees and brush to improve a site, so you're stuck with what's available and your own ingenuity in weather-proofing your tent.

About the only advice worth repeating is don't camp in a meadow or mossy area or near dead-standing trees. Cold damp air settles in meadows, and moss traps rain like a giant sponge. Midwestern loggers call dead-standing trees "widow-makers." Can you guess why?

A GroundCloth Inside Your Tent

As mentioned in the last chapter, even well-sealed seams will admit water in prolonged rain. And no tent floor will remain watertight forever. The solution is to always use a plastic groundcloth *inside* your tent. Water which wicks into your tent through worn floor seams and fabric will be trapped *beneath* the interior groundsheet, and you'll stay dry.

Except when snow camping (to prevent the floor from freezing to the ground) *never* place the groundsheet under the tent floor. Water will become trapped between the groundsheet and floor and be pressure-wicked by body weight into the sleeping compartment. You'll really have a sponge party if this happens.

Rig For Wind

The best turn-of the-century A-frame tents were better foul weather shelters than modern campers like to admit. Studying one reveals some interesting things about where to place seams, guylines, and stake points. Let's check out one of these canvas antiques.

- There's a single vertical pole at each end. The poles are located at the apex of the triangular door and back wall. In essence, they form the "altitude" of each triangle.
- The tent has no floor, so there are no perimeter seams at ground level. A removable, rubberized ground-sheet, placed inside, protects occupants from flowing ground water and dampness.
- Including the corners, there are *five* stake points per side hem. A center stake halves the length of the sidewall material; the other splits the distance between adjacent stakes. There's that "apex-of-the-triangle" relationship again.
- Guylines at each end originate on the poles, or at heavily reinforced fabric very near the poles. The exoskeleton—not the fabric—absorbs most of the wind stress.

Rigging storm lines is largely a game of triangles. Locate an apex, put in a stake or guyline. This keeps fabric tight by equalizing strain. As any elk hunter will attest, a modern canvas wall tent will withstand quite a blow. That these tents perform much better than their simple geometry suggests is no mystery to those who use them.

Now, let's use what we've learned to undress America's most popular tent, the Eureka Timberline.

Tuning The Timberline

First, the "hem" test. Does the fly cover all exposed perimeter seams? You bet! At least along the sidewalls. The Timberline has a full bathtub floor, so fly coverage below the elevated bathtub seams isn't necessary, right?

Wrong! Fabrics wear, and the floor sidewalls are no exception. An extra waterproof layer here is always a plus. Seam coverage on the Timberline is adequate for vertical rain but not for wind-driven weather.

Rule: If your tent has exposed stitching or a fly that can be blown aside by high winds, you'll need to extend the fly by sewing on matching material. Make cuts above stake and guyline loops so you won't have to re-attach them to the new fabric.

Move to the corners where the toggle pins plug into the pole ends and note that some corner stitching is exposed to the weather. You'll have to rely on glue (seam-sealant) here—a bad idea. Or you can solve the problem instantly by attaching a vestibule to one or both ends of the tent. Adding a vestibule is the easiest way to weatherproof the entry of any tent.

Check out the hems along the sidewalls. There are just two equidistant stake points, neither of which splits the distance between tent corners. The result is that a strong side wind can compress the center sidewall hem into the porous canopy. Correcting the problem is easy; just sew a third stake loop to the hem center at point "a" (see figure 5-1). Note how this one center stake firms the sidewall.

The Timberline is a comfortable, relatively high tent, with lots of sidewall exposed to the wind. Stiffen each wall by sewing a nylon storm loop to the center of the fly at point "b" of figure 5-1. Be sure to back with heavy fabric whatever you sew.

The aluminum A-frame is your final concern. Standard issue Timberline poles simply aren't designed for winds above 30 miles an hour. (The expedition poles are much sturdier.) Is there a way to stiffen the framework without adding weight or bulk?

You bet! Sew a nylon guy loop to the fly face at the mid-point of each pole which makes up the A-frame. Back the loop on the inside fly with a length of mating Velcro.

When the weather gets nasty, secure the Velcro tabs to the poles and guy the outside loops. Since the Velcro tabs secure directly to the poles, there is no stress on the fly fabric—and no danger of tearing it.

Rule: Whenever possible, guy off the framework rather than the tent fabric.

Now, apply this philosophy to each end of the tent. The Timberline is effectively "freestanding;" there are no forward and aft guylines to provide stability in oncoming winds. To account for this, the manufacturer has provided a D-ring on the ridge at each end. You can attach guy lines directly to these, right?

Wrong! Re-read the RULE above and you'll see why. The first good blast of air will tear the D-rings right off the tent. There's a better way.

1. Sew a Velcro tab to the underside of the fly, opposite the D-ring. Secure the tab to the plastic pole junction tube, then guy off the D-ring.
2. Or disregard the D-ring and secure your guyline(s) directly to the horizontal junction tubes, as illustrated in figure 5-1. If possible, attach guy and stake lines to an immovable object like a tree or rock. Otherwise, use two tent stakes per loop and weight the stakes with rocks or logs so they won't pull out if the soil turns to mud.

Tip: Attach 3-foot lengths of parachute cord to each stake loop. When the ground is too hard for staking, wrap each cord around a stick and pile rocks on top, or use multiple shallow running stakes. You'll reduce stress on tent fittings if you add loops of shock-cord to all guylines.

Waterproof Tent Seams

In the last chapter, I suggested that you waterproof tent seams with Thompson's Water Seal or other commercial compound. Sealing seams helps, but frankly, it's mostly window dressing. If your tent fly covers every seam and zipper, you can eliminate this step. That's because rain which gets through stitching on the fly will, due to surface tension, slither harmlessly to the ground. There is no particular advantage in sealing floor seams if you use a groundcloth inside your tent.

Let's review the rules for stormproofing tents:

1. Perimeter floor seams (there should be none) must be fully covered by the tent fly. Check the tent corners. If there's a problem here, adding a vestibule may solve it. If not, sew on an extension of some sort.
2. There should be enough stake points (you can never have too many) along the fly hem to prevent wind-whipped rain from getting under the fly and onto seams. If your tent needs more stake points, add them.
3. High-walled tents can be stabilized by attaching a guyline to the center face of the fly. Back your sewing with extra material. Don't run a canopy "pull-out" cord from the inner fly face to the canopy to increase space inside the tent. Rain will wick through the stitching on the fly face and slither down the side-pull into the sleeping compartment. If your tent already has a canopy side-pull, disconnect it the moment rain begins. If this is impractical, tie a cotton shoelace or handkerchief to the cord somewhere between the fly and canopy. Now any water that wicks through will follow the hanky to the ground (at least for a while) rather than into your tent.
4. Whenever possible, guy directly off the framework of a tent. If you must attach lines to fabric, back what you sew with heavy material.

Now, stand back and take a long, proud look at your accomplishments. You have a tent that will keep you dry in any rain. Cost of materials? Under ten dollars. Time involved? About three hours.

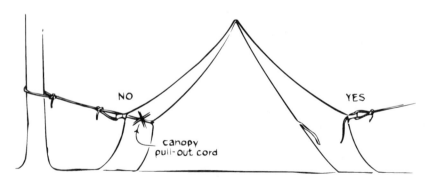

Figure 5-2   *Disconect "canopy pull-out" cords in rain!*

6. CLASSIC TENTS YOU CAN MAKE

In the fifties, when I was a boy scout, I owned a Spartan 5' x 7' canvas "wedge" tent. There were no zippers, bug nets, or windows, and no floor. A rubberized poncho doubled as a ground-cloth, and in buggy weather I wore a head net. With two wooden poles and ten stakes, the little pup tent weighed exactly 7 pounds—a respectable weight for a hiking tent, even by today's standards.

Figure 6-1a *Wedge Tent, closed.*

I used the wedgie in all types of weather—backpacked all over upper Michigan with it—and can recall only one time when I was wet and cold. It was my "go light" philosophy and a cold, two-day rain that did me in. I got just what I deserved when I placed my dry sleeping bag on top of my wet poncho. From then on, I carried a special groundcloth for use inside my tent.

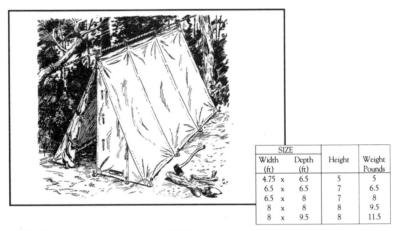

| SIZE | | Height | Weight |
Width (ft)	Depth (ft)		Pounds
4.75 x	6.5	5	5
6.5 x	6.5	7	6.5
6.5 x	8	7	8
8 x	8	8	9.5
8 x	9.5	8	11.5

Figure 6-1b *Canvas wedge tent, circa 1912*

In the sixties, I bought my first nylon backpacking tent—a "three man" Gerry Fireside. More commodious and half the weight of the wedge, it featured true double-walled (waterproof fly over porous canopy) construction. The Gerry had a window in back and an integral floor and bug net. Man was I living! For more than a decade, the little tent was a constant companion on canoe camping trips in Minnesota and Canada. It never failed me in any weather.

Though I now own more sophisticated tents, I continue to use the Gerry for solo canoeing. Admittedly, my other tents are "geometrically better," but none are lighter, more compact, and faster to pitch. With its built-in (sewn to the ridge) rain-fly and shock-corded I-poles, the Fireside goes up in less than a minute. Few modern tents can do as well.

Admittedly, for high altitude and severe weather use, state-of-the-art tents outshine the old-timers by a wide margin. But for general camping in forested areas, many turn-of-the-century tents are better. At any rate, the best of the nostalgic designs were lighter, better ventilated, and roomier than most people think.

Many of the old tents—like the "wall", "wedge", "baker", and "forester"—are still in production. Attempts to modernize these designs by substituting nylon for canvas have generally been unsuccessful. That's because "breathable" canvas still is the best material (and certainly the most durable) for large, airy tents. Though I spent considerable time "under canvas" when I was a kid, I now prefer nylon tents by a wide margin. Nonetheless, the traditional tents of the past have much to recommend them. Reproduced here from the 1912 Abercrombie Camp catalog are four of the most popular models for your interest and amusement. Study the specifications, and you'll discover how light and versatile these shelters were. You may even want to build one yourself. Plans for the simplest models are included for your convenience.

Wedge Tent

Simplest of all designs, the wedge is versatile and cozy. When constructed with a doorway at each end, the structure can be opened to face a fire. Snap or Velcro a mosquito bar to the roof, and you have a tent that is similar to the "convertible A-tent" recommended by the legendary outdoorsman, Calvin Rutstrum, in his book, *The New Way of the Wilderness*. The design is so simple you can easily draw your own plans from the specifications.

Note: A twin door version of this classic tent is manufactured in mildew-resistant army duck by TENTSMITHS, Box 496, North Conway, NH 03860.

Foresters' Tent

This ultralight tent was designed around 1910, by Field & Stream's editor, Warren Miller. Nothing more than a tapered tarp, the Forester goes up fast on any terrain and is very wind-resistant. The 1912 Abercrombie catalog lists a weight of just 2 3/4 pounds for the 8' x 8' version—this, in cotton canvas. Try finding a two person *nylon* tent that light today!

Build a campfire out front, and you'll discover how well the cone-shaped entrance funnels heat to the occupants inside. The Forester was a standard offering in Boy Scout catalogs for nearly 50 years. David Abercrombie writes about the material used in this and other Abercrombie manufactured tents:

"The cloth is treated by a copper process which makes it waterproof, rot proof and vermin proof, and leaves it perfectly pliable and soft. Even the

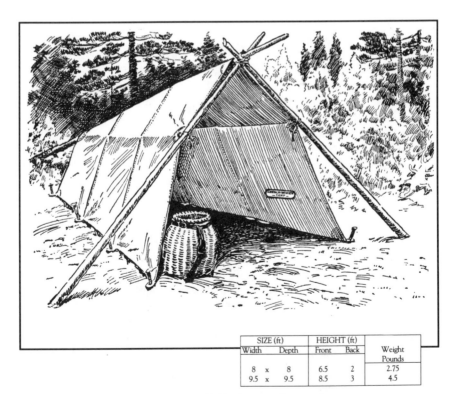

SIZE (ft)		HEIGHT (ft)		Weight Pounds
Width	Depth	Front	Back	
8 x	8	6.5	2	2.75
9.5 x	9.5	8.5	3	4.5

Figure 6-2a *Foresters' Tent, from 1912 Abercrombie catalog.*

white ant will not attack it; neither does it burn as readily as unprocessed material and it is not affected by either tropic heat or Arctic cold, changes in temperature making little differences in its feeling.

It is a non-conductor of heat, which makes it a cool summer and a warm winter tent. The color is a great advantage, the green being a shade that is easy for the eyes and flies and gnats are not so troublesome in a green tent."

from CAMP OUTFITS

David T. Abercrombie Company, New York, NY, 1912

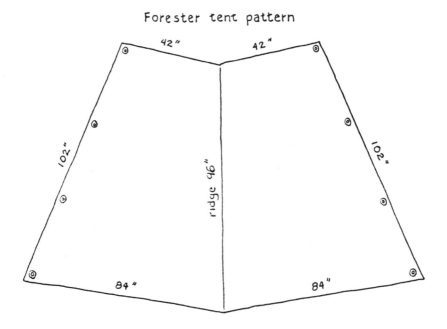

Figure 6-2b

Baker Tent

Everyone who has camped out for very long eventually comes to know and love the Baker tent. Guy out the fly and build a cheery fire beneath; gather the crew and deal the cards. There's room enough for all, even when heavy rain blows up. Add a sod cloth, bug net, side wings, and a privacy screen out front, and you have a snug four season shelter that's as much at home in Patagonia as at a friendly KOA campground. Baker tents once were the backbone of every nineteenth-century hunting camp, and in parts of the American west, they remain so today. Note that CAMP OUTFITS lists the 8' x 6 1/2' model at just 9 pounds—lighter even than the popular nylon Eureka Timberline.

You can buy a modern baker tent from TENTSMITHS and many western outfitters.

SIZE (ft)		HEIGHT (ft)		
Width	Depth	Front	Back	Weight Pounds
6.5 x	3.25	4	1	3.5
6.5 x	6.5	5	1.5	7
8 x	6.5	6	2	9
9.5 x	8	7	2.5	13.5

Figure 6-3   *Baker tent, from 1912 Abercrombie catalog.*

Miners' Tent

When it comes to efficient utilization of space, the Miners' tent is hard to beat. Four pegs and a tie at the top (or interior pole) stabilize this tent in winds that would flatten most conventional designs. Spread the door flaps and feel the heat of your campfire. Button up tight, and listen to the patter of rain while you stay dry inside. The Miner is great for winter camping too; just run the pipe of your sheet-metal stove through a thimble in the roof and watch things heat up fast inside.

Pyramid tents like these were popular in the cowboy days and well into this century. Journals of the early Arctic explorers praised the Miner tent for its light weight, wind stability, and ease-of-pitching.

SIZE (ft)		Height (ft)	Weight
Width	Depth		Pounds
6.5 x	6.5	6.5	5
8 x	8	7.5	6.75
9.5 x	9.5	8.5	9.75

Figure 6-4   *Miners' tent, from 1912 Abercrombie catalog.*

Whelen Lean-To

The Whelen Lean-to was designed by the famous outdoorsman, Colonel Townsend Whelen. A retired army officer, Colonel Whelen wrote prolifically about guns, hunting, and camping. Even when it was no longer fashionable, he preferred to base his hunts out of tents rather than RV's or motels. Whelen disliked the popular campfire tents of the day because their sloping backwalls reflected campfire heat onto the floor rather than the occupants. And everyone had to sleep with his head or feet towards the fire, which cooked one end and froze the other. "Much smarter to sleep sideways, so all parts get done at once," snipped the Colonel.

Whelen added a short vertical wall to the back of a conventional lean-to, then he sewed on a generous awning and side-flaps. Voila! The Whelen Lean-to was born. It's interesting to note that Eureka recently introduced a facsimile of this still popular 1926 design—in waterproof nylon, of course.

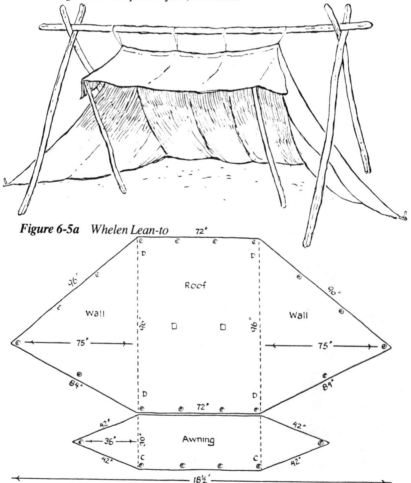

Figure 6-5a   *Whelen Lean-to*

Figure 6-5b   *Plans for building*

7. PERSONAL SURVIVAL SHELTERS

Everyone who has spent much time in the woods has, at one time or another, become lost. In his memoirs, Daniel Boone tells how he once became "mightly confused" for three days. As a young forester, I once shared a similar experience while working in western Oregon for the Bureau of Land Management. I did an incredibly stupid thing—one which I am naturally embarrassed to share with readers. But I was barely 21 at the time, so I'll blame my incoherence on youth.

I'd just finished marking a timber sale near Coos Bay when I was told the sale was cancelled. My instructions were to remove the yellow plastic ribbon from the trees which denoted the cutting line. Now, most people of normal intelligence would simply follow the flagging to the end, then remove it. Not me. I began picking ribbons off the trees the moment I entered the woods. To my credit, I realized the folly of this almost immediately, but I nonetheless persisted. After all, I'd established the cutting line, which for the most part, followed a ridge. Yeah, there were some crossovers, but these were "obvious." I was certain I wouldn't get lost.

By noon that day, I was "mightly confused." By dark, I was hopelessly lost. Sure, I knew the rules: stay put, build a fire and someone will find you. But it was *Friday*, and the government doesn't work on weekends. Monday was a holiday and I had Tuesday off for elk hunting. No one would even think of looking for me till Wednesday—five days from now. Besides, this was the Pacific Coast Range, where Douglas Fir trees grow tall as skyscrapers. Crown cover here was close to 100 percent. Even a combat chopper pilot couldn't spot me beneath all that foliage. And making a signal fire in the persistent December rain was out of the question. Suddenly, "survival" became a meaningful word.

Space does not permit sharing the details of my ordeal. Suffice it to say that I set my compass for due west—direction of the ocean and Highway 101—and struck

41

off into the rain-drenched forest. Clothed in woolens and waterproof rain gear, I also had a knife, cigarette lighter, Thermos of coffee, and my lunch. Water abounded everywhere.

Three days later I walked into the sunlight of an unimproved logging road, which I followed to the whistle stop town of Remote, Oregon. From there, I hitched a ride back to my Jeep. I never told BLM about my adventure. Why? Because foresters *don't get lost.*

In this chapter, we'll examine some personal survival shelters and techniques for coping with a wilderness emergency. You'll find no energy-draining, thatched roof lean-to's that take hours to build, for when you are lost, food is at a premium. Better to keep things simple by modifying natural shelters (caves, downed trees, brush piles, etc.) to meet your needs.

Frankly, a positive mental attitude (PMA) is your most important survival tool. I vividly remember praising my Silva compass at the end of my three day ordeal. Without it—and the knowledge to go west—I probably would have died in the Oregon woods, shelter or no. The "tools of survival" are less important than believing you'll get out alive.

Shelters

As you learned from chapter 3, the possibilities are endless if you have a tarp. If not, the rule is to modify an existing shelter. Can you remove the lower branches of a downed tree to create a small nest? Or burrow into the hollow at its base? Perhaps you can stack some brush or logs along one side to block out the wind. A tiny reflector fire will help you weather the storm.

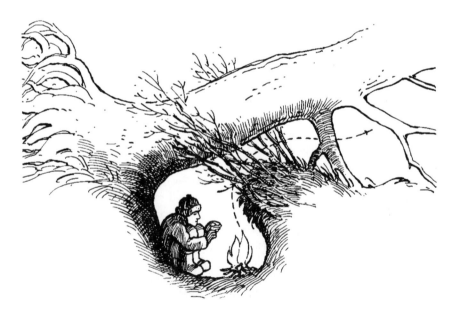

Figure 7-1   *Natural downed tree shelter.*

Before you move in, check for potential dangers—dead trees that may blow down on you, loose rocks, dry wash, etc. Make your crawl space large enough to stretch out but small enough to conserve heat.

Next comes bark or boughs to insulate the floor and walls. If it's raining, divert the water with make-shift guttering. Otherwise, shingle fresh cut browse. This is no time to think environmentally: cutting vegetation and trenching your home are a tenet of survival.

Now, crawl inside and try the fit. If you're cold, use evergreen boughs or leaves for a blanket. Perhaps if you rearrange the layering of your clothes you will add some warmth. For example, suppose you're wearing (from the skin out) cotton tee shirt, cotton-polyester long-sleeved shirt, wool sweater. Cotton wicks away body heat at a rapid pace, while wool does not. So wear your sweater next to the skin and the cotton garments over it. Don't overlook the value of non-traditional insulation like newspaper, leaves, life jacket, or your packsack. Rope, coiled about your body, will even provide warmth.

If you have a vehicle, you have lots of options. All you have to do is dissect the expensive upholstery and sew the pieces into clothing. Any sharp object will function as an awl. Fabric ravelings and electrical wire provide thread (have you tried dental floss?), sticks become buttons. No formulas; just ingenuity.

Survival Kit

Most commercial survival kits have cutesy items like wire, fish hooks, bandaids, and safety pins that you will never use. The result is a heavy, bulky unit that's more likely to be left at home than carried to the wilds. At the other extreme are impractical belt-size kits whose miniaturized components defy productive use. For example, one enterprising company offers a wallet-sized "survival card" that comes with a magnetized disk (compass?) which points north when you float it in water. How absurd!

The kit illustrated in figure 7-2 is recommended by the Minnesota Department of Natural Resources. There is at least one documented case where quick thinking and some of its components saved a life. Here's the story.

A Minneapolis teenager was snowmobiling when a blizzard created white-out conditions. Fortunately, the boy had recently completed an outdoor education class in high school, and he had a simple survival kit in his possession. When the young man could no longer see to drive, he used the coffee can to scoop snow from under the machine. Then he put on the plastic bag "rain suit," wrapped himself in the space blanket, and spent the night inside the hollow. His snowmobile suit kept him warm, the "rain suit" kept him dry, and the reflective space blanket helped retain body heat. Here are the contents of his survival kit, along with some proven extras.

Suggested Survival Kit Contents

1. Two large "leaf and lawn size" plastic bags. Cut out the bottoms and duct tape them together to form a continuous tube which can double as a "tent" and "rain suit."
2. Space blanket. Get one of the compact versions at any outdoor store. Don't open it; you'll never fit it back into the container. These space

small plastic
whistle

space
blanket

plumbers
candle

large
bandana

25 foot
nylon line

all go in
a two lb
coffee can
container

15-20
matches

2 large
leaf-size
plastic bags

small
mirror

2 large
Zip-loc bags

pocket
Knife

fire-starter

Figure 7-2 Survival kit

blankets are actually too small to cover an adult. Best use them to supplement your trash bags or to help warm a victim of hypothermia.

3. 15-20 wooden stick matches, a large plumbers candle (which will burn for hours), and a solid fuel chemical fire-starter, (which will enable anyone to make a blaze in any weather).

4. If space permits, bullion cubes, tea and sugar. Be aware, however, that food is a low priority item when you're lost. Your main concern is shelter, warmth, and *getting found.*

5. A one-pound coffee can with fitted plastic lid (which makes a handy pot, snow shovel, and container for everything).

6. A whistle (the new pea-less designs take up little space) and small mirror for signaling.

7. Two Zip-lock bags. Use them as a cold weather vapor barrier (wear them against the skin) on your feet or hands and as a container for berries, minnows, tinder, etc.

8. 25 feet of strong nylon line (which suspends your "tube tent" from trees or becomes a belt to secure your "rain gear"). Warning: *Never* seal the ends of a non-porous, plastic tube tent. Doing so could cause suffocation.

9. Large cotton bandanna. (which doubles as a neck-warmer, sun and bug hat, cravat bandage, and spare sock). Use it to strain minnows and crawfish.

10. Small, single-bladed knife. A razor blade is no substitute for a sharp knife. If you include a compass in your kit, make it real one. The Silva Huntsman is the most compact, accurate instrument available.

Pack everything in the tin can and seal the lid with several feet of duct tape, which you can use to rig shelters and mend holes in plastic bags.

8. SNOW SHELTERS

It's a well-kept secret that winter camping is a whopping good time. After all, when it's 20 below, only fools and "them's that knows what they're about" are apt to be out there. Along with predictable solitude comes exquisite beauty and awesome silence. Camped on a pristine blanket of white, there are no foot prints or garbage to muck up the view. Touch the crispness of dawn, hear the harsh stillness of night. Like those who lived here millennia ago, you are part of the land, not meaningless passersby. What was in summer is no more. Everything is covered by sterile white.

Getting around in 4-foot snow drifts requires new technique. You shuffle along on snowshoes or glide on skis. Equipment is carried in special backpacks or on classic toboggans, polyethylene sleds, or fiberglass pulks. Fire building becomes an art as well as a lesson in tedium. First, you establish a base of logs so flames won't sink into oblivion; then, you split dry kindling from the heart of a snow-drenched log. A folding saw and axe and a good sharp knife are essential tools in the winter woods.

And if you go above the tree line, there are new challenges and equipment. Instead of fires there are gasoline and butane stoves, low slung mountain tents with cook-holes and tunnel doors, baffled parkas, balaclava's and face masks, vapor barrier liners, tinted goggles, and frost cream. And when tents fail—or for those who just disdain them—there are snow caves and trenches, Quin-zees and igloos. To the uninitiated, "sleeping out" in the dead of winter flirts with death. To those of us who know and live by nature's rules, it's hyacinths for the soul.

Ask an experienced winter camper if he or she prefers unheated tents to snow houses, and you'll get ten to one in favor of the huts. That's because unlike tents, snow structures are warm inside. Sometimes too warm. Everyone knows that snow is a great insulator, but you won't believe how good until you've crammed three people into a snow cave built for two. Add a candle or two for light and warmth, and watch

46

the thermometer rise. Keep a close eye on the mercury level, for when water starts dripping from the inner walls, you've got problems. Snow is porous, but ice doesn't breathe. And if your home freezes solid inside, air won't get in. Overheating a snow house is a very real concern—one which newcomers to winter sport don't take seriously enough.

Warnings aside, snow huts are comfortable and eminently safe, and as every kid will attest, they are fun and easy to build. Here are some ideas to get you started.

Building a Quin-zee Hut

Quin-zee or snow cave, the principle is the same. With a cave, you burrow into a ready made snowdrift and carve it to your dimensions. To build a Quin-zee, you make a giant snow pile then shovel out the inside, leaving a foot thick shell. The snow pile structure is no work of art, but it is as sturdy and spacious as an Eskimo igloo. You don't need a thick layer of snow to build a Quin-zee. You can haul in what you need or scrape a thin surface layer of snow from a frozen lake.

A 12-foot diameter size is about right for two. Err on the large side and adjust interior dimensions when you dig out the structure. Pile snow about 7-feet high, then "porcupine" the pile with foot long sticks all around. Don't stop until the Quin-zee resembles a medieval mace. These sticks gauge the wall thickness (which should be at least 8-inches) so you won't break through when you dig out the center.

Next comes the hard part—finding something to do for a few hours while the snow settles. How long this takes depends on temperature, humidity, and age of the snow. The warmer the day, the faster the molecular change. Eight hours is usually sufficient in any weather. *Do not* throw water on the hut to speed curing: you'll wind up with a giant ice ball—one you can't dig out of or breathe inside.

When the structure has hardened, dig out the center. A large coffee can makes a good shovel for sculpting the interior. Remove one of the porcupine sticks to make a vent hole on top. The others should remain in place. Don't panic if the vent fills with snow and closes. You'll get plenty of fresh air through the doorway and porous walls of the hut.

If you constructed a tunnel entrance to break the wind, you don't need a door. Otherwise, an angled snow block will reduce heat loss without affecting ventilation.

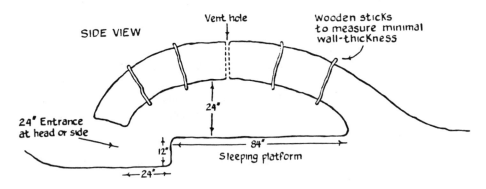

Figure 8-1   Quin-zee hut

Be sure you don't close the snow block door completely.

Caution: Always place the door of a Quin-zee or snow cave on the windward side of the structure. If wind-driven snow begins while you sleep, enough snow could accumulate on the leeward side of the hut to seal a down-wind entrance. This could be quite serious in a blizzard. Always keep a small shovel in any snow structure in case you need to dig out in the morning.

Tip: Nylon parachute cord makes an acceptable knife for cutting blocks from "old" snow. Just saw the cord back and forth until the block is free.

Sleeping in the Quin-zee

Warm air rises, cold air falls—a principle which explains why the floor of a Quin-zee is elevated a foot or more above the entrance. The heat generated by two bodies in a small hut will easily maintain near freezing temperatures inside even when it's 30 below outside. As stated, the danger is not in being too cold; it is allowing the structure to overheat and melt. So watch your thermometer: 20 degrees Fahrenheit is a good, safe temperature to maintain.

Given such balmy living conditions, a standard three-season sleeping bag is all you need for warmth. The key is to have plenty of insulation below. You're sleeping on ice, remember?

On top of your plastic ground cloth, place a minimum 2-inch thick, open-cell foam pad or a 5/8-inch thick, closed cell foam pad. If you choose an air/foam mattress, like the popular Thermarest, carry a repair kit or an extra pad in case it fails. Non-insulated air mattresses of any type are unsuitable for sleeping on snow.

Fears

Some people are afraid of carbon-monoxide poisoning, which is ridiculous, considering the generously sized door, vent hole, and porous walls.

As to the hut collapsing on you, forget it. Snow huts are incredibly strong, and they become stronger with age. You could probably drive a car over a week old Quin-zee without crushing it.

Tip: If you plan to use the shelter for several nights, chip away the ice build-up on the inner walls each day. This will maintain the breathability of the structure.

One Person Trench Shelter

You can use your nylon tarp in a variety of creative ways to construct a trench shelter. One plan is illustrated in figure 8-2.

1. Make a snow pile 6 x 12 x 3 feet deep. Like the Quin-zee, let it set awhile before you begin the process of digging out. If you can find a snow drift of these dimensions, you may begin digging immediately.

2. Dig a trench 9-feet long, 3-feet wide, and 2-feet deep. Make the entrance a foot lower than the sleeping platform so cold air will be be drawn out of the structure.

3. Span the structure (side-to-side) with a couple dozen, closely spaced sticks. Then set your tarp over the cross-bars and cover it with an insulating layer of snow.

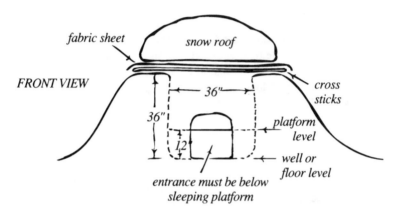

FRONT VIEW

fabric sheet

snow roof

cross sticks

36"

36"

12"

platform level

well or floor level

entrance must be below sleeping platform

TOP VIEW

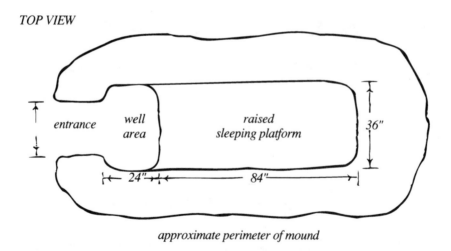

entrance

well area

raised sleeping platform

36"

24"

84"

approximate perimeter of mound

Figure 8-2 *Trench shelter*

Tip: You won't need cross-sticks if you substitute two seven foot long aluminized space blankets for your nylon tarp. Merely overlap the cold-stiffened space blankets so they'll cover the 9-foot trench, then anchor the sides with snow. A real advantage of the space blankets over a conventional tarp is that they reflect *much more* warm rising air back to the sleeper below.

If you leave snow on your tarp overnight, the snow will compact and make the tarp difficult to remove in the morning. One solution is to allow the snow to set for a few hours, then pull out the sticks and remove the tarp from inside the trench (better have smooth sticks or you'll tear the tarp). Expect some falling snow, but the roof should hold. Like a Quin-zee, it will grow stronger with time.

Vaulted Roof Snow Trench

If you have a snow knife (machete) and "old snow," you can build a vaulted roof like that shown in figure 8-3. Be sure to cut the blocks long enough so they'll butt at the peak. Fill cracks with loose snow.

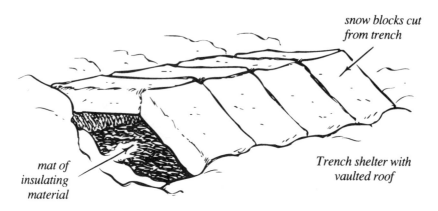

snow blocks cut
from trench

mat of
insulating
material

Trench shelter with
vaulted roof

Figure 8-3 *Valuted roof snow trench.*

Sleeping Out In Winter

Sleeping out in winter requires extra preparation. As mentioned, you need substantial insulation under your sleeping bag. Here are some other tricks that will add to your comfort.

1. Place outer clothing in your sleeping bag before you retire. The clothes will absorb some of the bag's cold and reduce the size of the area your body must heat. Remove the clothing as the bag warms up.
2. Wear long johns, balaclava, and down or Polarguard™ booties to bed for extra warmth. *Don't* bring down parkas into your bag with you; they will absorb insensible perspiration and become damp.

3. If you eat some high energy food before you retire, your body will produce more heat as you sleep.

4. Make a "draft collar" for your sleeping bag by placing a wool sweater or scarf across your chest and neck. Tuck the sweater sleeves around your shoulders to prevent air loss at the head of the bag.

5. Don't cover your face with your sleeping bag if your nose gets cold. Your bag will not be able to eliminate the moisture from your breathing. It may even ice up on the outside—a dangerous situation. Instead, use a sweater or shirt as a face mask. You can easily breathe through this porous material.

6. A midnight urination call at 20 below is no fun. Carry a special poly bottle for elimination. Women may want to try the proven "Sani-fem™" device.

7. In winter, your sleeping bag cannot dissipate all the moisture your body produces, so air out your bag in the sunlight for several minutes each day.

8. A candle will raise the temperature of your tent or snow shelter by 10 or 20 degrees. Batteries don't work well when they're cold, so insulate them until they are needed. A head lamp with battery pack placed inside your parka works great.

9. Water bottles should be stored upside down so that freezing will occur at the air interface, not the cap. Your canteen won't freeze if you place it under the foot of your sleeping bag.

9. AND THE COMFORTS OF HOME

Newcomers to the sport of camping out reluctantly admit that they often have trouble getting a good night's sleep. Either the tent leaks, the site slopes, the ground is bumpy, or the bugs are bad. At this, old-timers simply roll their eyes in pretend concern and recant the usual solutions:

> ...the classic, traditional campsite is near stream or lake water, but not right on the shore. Up in the prevailing breezes, which have such salubrious effects as discouraging mosquitoes while keeping tent, bags and clothing well aired and dry. Wily old-timers try to catch a campsite that is sunny during the morning, yet shady in late afternoon. Try north and east of trees, a hill, or some such...Be far enough away to be safe and yet enjoy the long afternoon shadows.
> From the *Complete Book of Practical Camping*
> John Jobson

Have you ever seen a place like this?

Camping in most areas today is highly regulated. In the "near" wilderness of the Boundary Waters Canoe Area, White Mountains National Forest, and others, campsites are carefully defined. Invariably, there's a fire grate and box latrine. Tent sites are champagne-glass smooth and well used. It is unethical and illegal to remove or prune vegetation to "improve" the sleeping area. You generally have to make the best of what's there.

And frankly, the federal workers who put in "wilderness" campsites don't always have your best interests in mind. To prevent environmental degradation or preserve scenic views, they often establish tent sites deep in the buggy woods, in hollows (which may flood in a good rain), or on sloping rock out-croppings. Your mission is to make these spots liveable.

Camping in deep, untraveled wilderness presents new problems. More often than not, prospective spots are too small and brushy to contain a tent. And those that aren't are almost never level. Environmental concerns yawn out to leave things untouched, yet some slashing and trampling is necessary for a comfortable stay. The alternative—and one that environmentally-conscious travellers always take—is to move on in search of happier hunting grounds.

Nonetheless, when the light of day grows dim and you're dead tired and weary of looking, any vegetation-free, flat spot will do. Now comes the hard part—eeking out a good night's rest on what you would normally consider "scenery." What follows are some untraditional ways to turn vinegar into wine.

TUNE UP YOUR SLEEPING SYSTEM FOR HAPPY Z's

Figure 9-1

Coping With A Bumpy, Unlevel Site

Scenario: You're canoeing the Hudson's Bay low lands in northern Manitoba. Hours of searching for a campsite yields the same uninhabitable terrain—knee-high grass and tag alders on the mud flats, and impenetrable, wrist-thick spruce on the boggy highlands. Camping in either of these places will be a lesson in misery. But the sun is declining fast, what to do?

The mud flats are the only option. Select the highest spot you can find—level or not—and pitch your tent. *Do not cut any* vegetation, as suggested in old-time camping books. It's not a matter of environmental ethics, for alder and grass will return in force the next season no matter what you do. The issue here is comfort. The low-to-the-ground, sharp stubs you cut will puncture your tent floor and sleeping mat immediately. Better to "fold plant stems over"—lay them as flat as you can—and pitch your tent on top. Everything will smooth down when you climb inside and roll around. In fact, the springy floor may be quite comfortable.

What if the site slopes? The traditional advice is to pitch your tent with the head end high. However, if there's a substantial incline, you'll slide to the bottom of the tent with each move you make—a very uncomfortable situation.   On gentle slopes, simply level your bed by placing carefully folded spare clothes under the lower half of your sleeping mat. Severe inclines present more of a problem. Jack up your legs with clothes and your buttocks fall into a hollow—okay for sleeping on your back, but not on your side. The alternative is to pitch the tent at right angles to the slope then jack up the down-hill side of your bed with spare clothes. The idea of "leveling" a bad situation is new to most campers, yet it is easy enough. After all, you have plenty of materials on hand. Besides clothing and rain gear, you have a packsack and tarp, towel, wool hat and gloves—maybe a life jacket and fabric canoe cover. Any or all of these items can be carefully folded and placed under your bed.

Tuning Your Mattress

Air Mattresses

Air mattresses are passé with experienced campers, and for good reason. They require time and energy to inflate; they develop holes—many of which require ingenuity to find—and they don't insulate very well. Their two attributes are comfort and small packed size.

If you prefer an air mattress, choose a type which has individually inflatable tubes. One highly recommended Australian model has a nylon shell that contains a number of easily replaceable vinyl tubes. If one tube goes flat, the others will continue to support you. A spare tube rolls to fist size and weighs only a few ounces.

Place a thin, closed-cell foam pad on top of your air mattress and you'll stay warm in temperatures well below freezing. And, you won't slide off the slick nylon surface of the mattress while you sleep.

Self-inflatable Airfoam Pads

Self-inflatable airfoam pads like the popular Thermarest ™ and Equalizer™ are state-of-the-art for sleeping out. Nearly all experienced campers use them. Air-foam pads are nearly as comfortable as air mattresses, and they insulate almost as well as closed-cell foam pads of equal thickness. Varying the amount of air in the pad changes the thickness (insulation and comfort). Sounds wonderful, and it is, but they are a little slippery.

Mate the slick nylon surface of a sleeping bag with that of an air pad, and it's slither city. Unless the tent floor is dead level, you'll need brakes to keep from sliding off the pad. There are thick rubber bands you can buy for this purpose and rubbery goo that glues on, but neither works very well. Best solution is make a removable cotton cover for the pad which will stabilize it and protect it against punctures. Most important, the cotton shell will be luxuriously comfortable to sleep on. You'll especially appreciate the feel of cool cotton on hot nights, when sweat streams down your back.

Sew a strip of Velcro to the top of your cotton cover and attach a mating strip to your nylon clothes bag or sleeping bag stuff sack. Fill the stuff sack with carefully folded clothes (a down vest is ideal) and stick it to your trail matt. Now, you have a pillow that won't migrate to the opposite end of the tent while you sleep.

Open-Celled Foam Pads

In recent years, fabric-covered open-celled foam pads have lost ground to the popular Thermarest™ and Equalizer™. However, since there are no valves to fail or air to leak, they are more reliable (and economical) than air pads, and on reasonably smooth ground, nearly as comfortable. Unfortunately, many manufacturers cover their open-celled pads with slippery waterproof nylon that traps insensible perspiration in the foam. You don't need a waterproof bottom on your sleeping pad if you have (which you should) a plastic groundcloth inside your tent. I can't emphasize enough that mattress covers should be made of nearly pure cotton. Every other fabric falls short of expectations.

Closed-Cell Foam Pads

Closed-cell foam pads like those made from Ensolite™, polyethylene, and ethyl-vinyl-acetate (EVA) are fail-proof and have the highest "R" factor (for their thickness) of all trail pads. For winter use, where mattress failure can be dangerous, closed-cell foam pads are the logical choice. Comfort is irrelevant here as there is no such thing as bumpy or unlevel ground. You're sleeping on a self-leveling bed of fluffy white, remember?

Since closed-cell foam pads don't absorb water, many travelers tie them—rolled and unprotected—to the outside of their packs. This is a big mistake because the "cut cells" of the foam will absorb moisture which will be transmitted directly to your sleeping bag. RULE: Carry sleeping pads inside your pack or cover them with waterproof material!

Tip: To increase the insulative value ("R" factor) of your trail mattress, lay folded clothing underneath it.

Tip: Your sleeping bag should not touch the walls of your trail shelter. On cool nights water will condense on the surface of your sleeping bag and be drawn into the filling.

10. THE WARMTH OF FIRE

Everyone has known at least one trip where freezing rain began with the first footstep and didn't end until the long drive home. We're talking liquid ice balls—the kind that scare you half to death even when you know what you're doing and are dressed in the best foul-weather gear money can buy. At these times, good clothing is a matter of comfort, if not survival.

Later in camp, when your tent is up and you need a nylon hood over your thick wool hat to keep your ears from buzzing in the driving sleaze, you'll want a rip-roaring fire which reflects warmth deep inside your sloping rain tarp. Prepare the evening stew on your PEAK 1, if you choose, but cuddle round the flickering blaze with a cup of hot buttered rum[1], and you'll know the real joy of camping.

Though every camper professes the ability to ignite a cheery blaze in any weather, facts suggest otherwise. Government surveys reveal that one-fifth of backcountry travelers cannot make fire under "textbook perfect" conditions unless they have dry paper or chemical fire-starters. And when the weather turns really sour, fire-making becomes an elusive skill that only seasoned experts have mastered.

There is no "right way" to build a fire, but there are proven techniques. Here's one of them.

The Right Tools
Knife

My Swiss Army knife is a welcome companion on all my canoe trips. On occasion, I've used every tool except the knife, which is a poor substitute for a

---

[1] The basic recipe consists of a jigger of rum, tablespoon of white or brown sugar, dash of cinnamon, pat of margarine, and three-fourths cup of boiling water.

good fixed blade or well built-folder. If you have to whittle the heart out of a storm-soaked chunk of birch to reach the dry kindling inside, a Swiss knife won't cut it. You need something more substantial—either a thin-bladed sheath knife with 4 to 5-inch blade (my preference) or a sturdy folder with stainless steel pins and solid brass bolsters.

I've put a lot of miles on high grade stainless steel knives, but I much prefer good tool steel, even for knives which may get wet. Tool steel sharpens more easily than stainless, and it takes a keener edge. And it's easier to mill at the factory, too, which means it is less expensive to buy. Knives made of "surgical stainless steel" (used for throw away scalpels and forceps) are only a few cuts above well-made blades from the Bronze Age. For an all around working knife, you can't beat good, high-carbon tool steel. But like a fine gun or canoe paddle, you must be willing to pamper it a bit, as you would with any prize possession.

Saw

A saw is essential for making a rainy day fire. The collapsible aluminum frame, triangular models sold in camp shops and discount stores are only better than no saw at all. Better to carry a one piece steel bow saw than to rely on these flimsy contraptions.

Best camp saw I've found is a full stroke rectangular model called the Fast Bucksaw, which is built from hard maple and has a quickly replaceable 21-inch blade (it takes a standard hardware store blade) which rides between slippery polyethylene washers. Hardware is stainless steel, nickel-plated steel or aluminum. The saw locks so rigidly when assembled you'd swear it was one piece. Folded length is just 21 inches, and all parts snap together for carrying. It's available by mail from FAST BUCKSAW, 110 East Fifth St., Hastings, MN 55033.

Hand-Axe

You're tripping with a group of teenagers in early June, and for three days it has rained continuously. At night, the wind stops, but the rain doesn't. And the next day begins with more rain which gives way to penetrating droplets of ice cold fog. You're the trip leader. You've got wool and polypropylene and rain gear that works. The kids have cast-offs and cheapie rain suits. You've got sense enough to keep your gear dry; the kids don't. They leave tent doors open and weather flaps unzipped; they bring wet boots and gear into their tents and leave dry clothes outside. They crowd four or five to a tent so there's no way to escape sidewall condensation. Kids are kids, and kids get wet. You're the leader, and it's your job to dry them out. Try doing that with the heat of your gasoline stove.

To maintain a roaring fire that's large enough to dry the crew, you'll need plenty of dry wood—something not readily available in the dripping forest. Now, if you could just split sections of that foot-thick downed birch over there, you'd have plenty of dry heartwood. Thank God you had the good sense to bring your *hand axe*.

First, saw the dead birch log into 12-inch lengths. Cut one, 2-foot long section to function as a splitting maul.

Next, set the hand-axe lightly into the end grain of a sawn section. Grasp the handle firmly with both hands while your partner pounds the head on through with the log mallet. Similarly, quarter each splitting, the center of which should be bone dry. It's essential that you use the hand-axe only for splitting, *never* for chopping. Cutting chores are performed with the folding saw. This method ensures you'll never have an "ax-ident."

Some authorities insist on carrying a full size (28-inch handle) axe under the guise it is safer than a hatchet. Hardly! No matter how long the handle, there's always the chance a chopping tool will ricochet. On the other hand, a mallet-driven splitting wedge (hand-axe, used as suggested) cannot possibly slip and cut.

An alternative to a hatchet is the mini-maul (one-handed fireplace maul) or steel splitting wedge. A mini-maul—which is just 2 pounds heavier than a conventional hatchet—is big medicine for making fires on rainy days. A splitting wedge is light and compact but more dangerous when the mallet comes down.

Making The Fire

First, collect your "tinder." A handful of inch thick splittings will do. Now, set everything aside and prepare the fire base as follows.

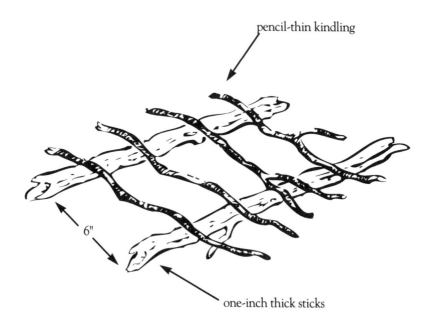

pencil-thin kindling

6"

one-inch thick sticks

Figure 10-1

Dig a hole about a foot in diameter and 6 inches deep (a foot-long aluminum tube with one end flattened makes a great shovel). Try to remove the sod in a single layer. Turn it dirt-side-up and pile your diggings on top.

Note: You can eliminate this step if you're making your fire on rock or in an approved fire grate.

Now, follow these steps:

Step One

Bridge the hole with a couple of inch thick splittings. Cut pencil-thin kindling and set it across the sticks.

Step Two

Stack long thin shavings or small dry twigs (tinder) about an inch high, atop your kindling supports. Leave plenty of space between each shaving. Smoke is nature's way of saying "you're smothering the flame!"

stack long thin shavings (tinder) *on top* of the kindling.

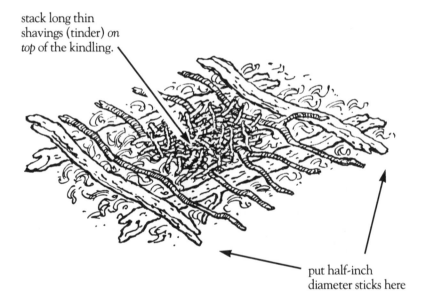

put half-inch diameter sticks here

Figure 10-2

Tip: To cut long, thin shavings instead of short, useless ones, use a "sawing" rather than whittling motion with your knife. Another trick is to reverse the blade—sharp edge in line with your wrist—and lock the pommel of the knife against your gut. Wedge the shaving stick outside the cutting edge as illustrated in figure 10-4, and wrench both arms smartly outward. This powerful method will produce a shedful of long, fine shavings in a matter of seconds.

Next, put two sticks, about as thick as your thumb, at right angles to the fire base. These will support the heavier kindling you'll add in step three.

Step Three

Now, slice some kindling *no thicker than a pencil* and criss-cross two or three tiers above your tinder box. This wood will burn fast and "lock" the shavings in place so wind won't blow them away. *Don't* heap a lot of wood on the fire right now. Too much fuel will rob the young fire of heat and oxygen and make it hard to start.

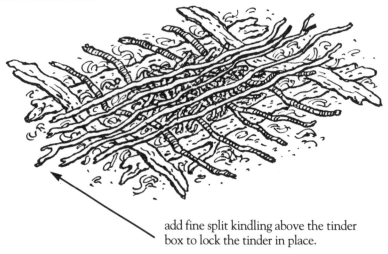

add fine split kindling above the tinder box to lock the tinder in place.

Figure 10-3

Lighting The Fire

Your fire is now ready for lighting. Note that the tinder box sits on a raised platform. Here's why: 1) Cold, damp ground will rob the fire of much of its heat during the early stages of combustion. 2) The platform permits a continuous draft, similar to that of a hibachi grill. 3) The raised fire base provides room to place a match directly under the flammable tinder.

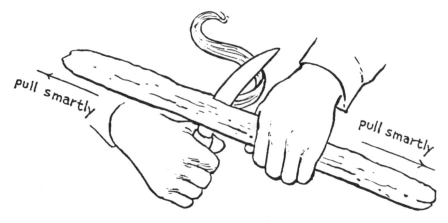

Figure 10-4 *Using a knife "backwards" to cut long, thin shavings.*

Clean-Up

You'll want to *leave no trace* of your camp, so burn every piece of wood *completely*. Then, bury the warm gray coals with the dirt you dug; fit the sod cap in place and smooth the area Boy Scout perfect.

Tip: A butane cigarette lighter, with adjustable flame, is handier than a match. However, do carry stick matches in case your lighter fails. A suitable watertight match case can be made by nesting a fired 16 gauge shotgun shell inside a 12-gauge shell. The dead primers of the shell casings provide a convenient striker.

Tip: Always carry a candle. Candles are necessary to provide the sustained heat required to ignite wet wood.

Tip: An effective method of drying matches is to draw them briskly through your hair. It's the static electricity that does the trick.

Tip: In the piney woods of the north and east, look for the balsam-fir tree, whose sap is as volatile as kerosine. In summer, the tree produces half-dollar sized resin blisters on its trunk. Lance a few blisters and collect the pitch on a piece of bark. Set your resin cup directly under your fire base and watch things heat up fast when you strike your match.

Let's review the rules for making a successful fire.

1. Place sticks far enough apart on the fire base so there'll be adequate ventilation for the developing flames. I suggest that you separate each stick by a distance equal to its radius. Remember, lack of oxygen is the major reason why fires fail.
2. Tinder should be wafer-thin—no thicker than the diameter of a match. Trying to ignite thick sticks on a damp day is an exercise in futility.
3. Don't heap the fire base high with wood during the developing stages of the flame. Unnecessary fuel draws heat from the young fire and cools it. Pre-set pyramid style fires (á la Boy Scouts) look nice in handbooks but burn inefficiently. Once you complete Step Three, wood should be added one stick at a time and placed strategically so that you can "see light" between each one. Smoke is nature's way of telling you you're suffocating the blaze.

Banking The Blaze

Some of my most memorable times as a boy scout were dozing off to sleep before the warmth and glow of a gently flickering fire. We wanted to keep these memories alive as long as possible, so we built a crisp, hot blaze, then "banked" it before we climbed into our sleeping bags. A well-banked fire will smolder all night long, even in light rain.

First, there's the matter of safety—yours and the forest's. Under no conditions should you ever bank a fire then retire to your tent. If a wind blows up, untended coals could evoke a raging forest fire. Banked fires are for rainy days and for open-faced shelters where they can be constantly watched.

The procedure for banking a fire follows:

1. Scoop all burnable material into the fire, then wall off three of the four sides of the fire place with rocks. If there is much wind, block the fourth side as well. The idea is to reduce the amount of oxygen to the bare minimum needed for burning. Clear all flammable debris away from the protective rock enclosure.
2. Place several wrist-thick logs, parallel to one another, across the fire. Space logs closely—no more than 1/2-inch apart. Again, the idea is to cut off most of the air. Now, your fire should safely smolder most of the night.

Use this modified banking procedure to dry wet wood and keep your fire alive in heavy rain:

1. Bridge two high rocks or logs with closely spaced, wrist-thick splittings. The split side of the logs should face the ground. Criss-cross several tiers of splittings over these.
2. Build your fire beneath this "ventilated" protective rain cover. As the fire burns, it will dry out the wood above, and your blaze will grow.

INDEX